Corporate and Financial Fraud

Corporate and Financial Fraud

a Wolters Kluwer business

Wolters Kluwer (UK) Limited
145 London Road
Kingston upon Thames
Surrey KT2 6SR
Tel: +44(0) 844 561 8166
Fax: +44(0) 208 247 1184
E-mail: customerservices@cch.co.uk
Website: www.cch.co.uk

© 2008 KPMG LLP, a UK limited liability partnership, is a subsidiary of KPMG Europe LLP and a member firm of the KPMG network of independent member firms affiliated with KPMG International, a Swiss cooperative.

ISBN: 978 1 84140 851 4

British Library Cataloguing-in-Publication Data

A catalogue record for this book is available from the British Library

Typeset by YHT Ltd
Printed and bound by Legoprint – Lavis (TN)

Preface

The aftermath of a fraud can be far more damaging than the incident itself. Financial loss is only one part of the ramifications; organisations can take years to recover from the damage, indeed some never do. Managers look back, trying to understand whether it could have been prevented. The answer is often 'yes', if only effective processes had been in place to prevent, detect and respond to fraud.

The experience of witnessing these situations has prompted this book, it is intended to be a highly practical look at understanding, identifying and reducing fraud risk. Much can be heard about corporate governance, risk management and internal control, but the concepts often become detached from the real-world financial disasters that inspired them. This book aims to put the reader back in touch with the reality of fraud.

Fraud is an underlying risk in every aspect of business life, and management should see combating it as one of their key objectives. The growth and spread of fraud in recent years, and the continuation of the managerial, financial and technological trends that have permitted that growth, leave no alternative to active engagement.

Since this is the third edition of this book (previous ones were published as *Fraud Watch*) it seems fair to assume that such a practical approach has filled a gap in the market. Nonetheless, because fraud is so fast changing – and business and professional life ever more demanding – we have made considerable changes. These include significant new material on understanding this type of criminal (with a particular focus on the 'insider' or white-collar fraudster), the causes of fraud, common indicators and risk factors, the threat from organised crime and a practical guide to fighting fraud.

This edition builds on much of the foundation laid by David Davies, a director at KPMG Forensic in the UK, who wrote the previous two editions and it is a tribute to him that so much of his material retains its value 15 years after he first put pen to paper.

I should also like to convey my gratitude to a number of other people from KPMG's UK firm for their part in preparing this new edition.

- Alex Plavsic, Partner in KPMG's Forensic practice, for his contributions to important aspects of the book, particularly that on fraud risk profiling which was originally written for *Risk Management and Internal Control* (published by GEE Publishing in 2000).

- Lesley Roberts, formerly Director of Information Security Management at KPMG, and Malcolm Marshall, Partner in KPMG's Information Risk Management practice, for writing the original chapter on IT fraud, together with Altaf Dossa, Senior Manager in KPMG's Forensic practice who has updated it.

- Roger Aldridge, Director in KPMG's Forensic practice, who provided content for the chapter on organised crime.

- David Eastwood, Partner in KPMG's Forensic practice who helped prepare information on fraud indicators; Gus MacKenzie, a Senior Manager, who helped by preparing the information on advance fee fraud; Danny McLaughlin, a Senior Manager in KPMG Forensic, who contributed to the previous editions; and Maninder Bahra, formerly of KPMG, who helped with the initial update of the work.

- Other present and former colleagues for their input to this and previous editions.

- Simon Pearce who provided editorial advice and assistance.

David Luijerink
London, July 2008

KPMG in the UK

Contents

1 The fundamentals

A serious fraud shakes any business to its core. The new 'black hole' in the results sends the share price plummeting. The chairman, chief executive and finance director prepare to resign. Staff bonuses are doomed and job losses are inevitable. The resulting fear and depression damages productivity and undermines the trust on which the business depends. Any manager concerned with internal control and audit risk may be tainted.

A nightmare scenario and one that happens not just to big names like Barings, Enron, WorldCom and Parmalat. Others frauds which did not make the headlines still left a trail of shredded equity, ruined careers and impoverished families. While not all organisations go bust when fraud occurs there are always victims.

History shows fraud can hit any organisation, usually for the same underlying, and preventable, reasons. The seeds of disaster may already be present in many companies, their chief officers unwittingly creating the conditions in which fraud will thrive.

As will become clear, it takes more than a criminal to make a fraud. Illusion and a failure to treat fraud professionally opens the door. Closing it requires a bracing sense of reality.

1.1 All about value

Lawyers have argued long and hard about defining fraud. Yet in business terms the definition is a straightforward one.

Fraud is any activity which ultimately drains value from another person or entity via dishonesty or deception.

It does not matter whether value is removed directly or indirectly, or whether or not the fraudster reaps a personal benefit. Whether he or she can be prosecuted is also a secondary consideration.

This common-sense, business-oriented definition embraces the whole range of fraud from gross mismanagement involving deception, to unauthorised risk taking, irregularities, manipulation and outright theft of assets.

1

It is important to emphasise that loss of value can mean more than immediate financial loss. For instance, though a misstatement in the accounts need not involve theft it will still impact adversely on an organisation because false data makes it harder to make the appropriate decisions.

The Fraud Act 2006 brought British law in line with this value-based definition. It creates a specific offence of fraud expressed in three categories: fraud by false representation, fraud by failure to disclose information, and fraud by abuse of position. It is no longer necessary to prove that the defendant gained by the fraud or that the victim suffered a material loss. An intention to cause loss by deception is now the criterion for criminal conviction.

1.2   Modelling reality

Good technique and the best technology will fail to save the day if faulty ideas lead to muddled thinking. It is vital to get a good understanding of the problem and develop an appropriate response from the outset.

Current business risk-management models often omit consideration of fraud or include it as a minor sub-category of operational risk. The more obvious types (such as payment fraud and stock loss) may be covered, but more pervasive issues such as accounts manipulation, dealing fraud, management or purchasing fraud are usually ignored.

A fundamental, if unspoken, assumption underlies these approaches to risk: that the majority of people are honest. It is uncomfortable to admit otherwise and some companies actively suppress any use of the word 'fraud' because it does not fit with their policy of 'empowerment' and 'trust'.

Focusing on the latest risk-management fashion, or for that matter the latest type of swindle, prevents us from really understanding fraud. It is important to identify the underlying elements rather than being distracted by novelty. There is no end to what we can discover from what some dismiss as yesterday's news.

1. *Dishonesty is endemic.* Fraud can occur if opportunity beckons and potential rewards exceed likely risks. This is not to deny that most people really are honest; it is simply a statement of fact confirmed by everyday experience.

2. *The most damaging frauds are inside jobs* and the worst are far more likely to be perpetrated by management than the rank and file. The more highly placed the employee the easier he or she will find it to

2 Why fraud is allowed to happen

It is possible to prevent fraud when what drives it is known. Yet far too few companies understand those deeper causes. Greed is at the root of much of it, but that is far from the whole story. Other factors create the opportunities which greed exploits and it is possible to influence these.

These factors include growth without appropriate oversight, a weak ethical environment or culture, the perverse incentives created by different types of remuneration and reward, the seemingly mundane matter of how a company is structured and – most serious in day-to-day terms – gaps in risk management. This chapter looks at stimulants to fraud and illustrates them via a range of real-life case studies while chapter 3 looks at understanding white-collar fraudsters.

Figure 2.1 shows some of the issues involved and is used throughout this chapter to help illustrate how they were prevalent or relevant factors in the various case studies.

Figure 2.1 Business and fraud risk management issues

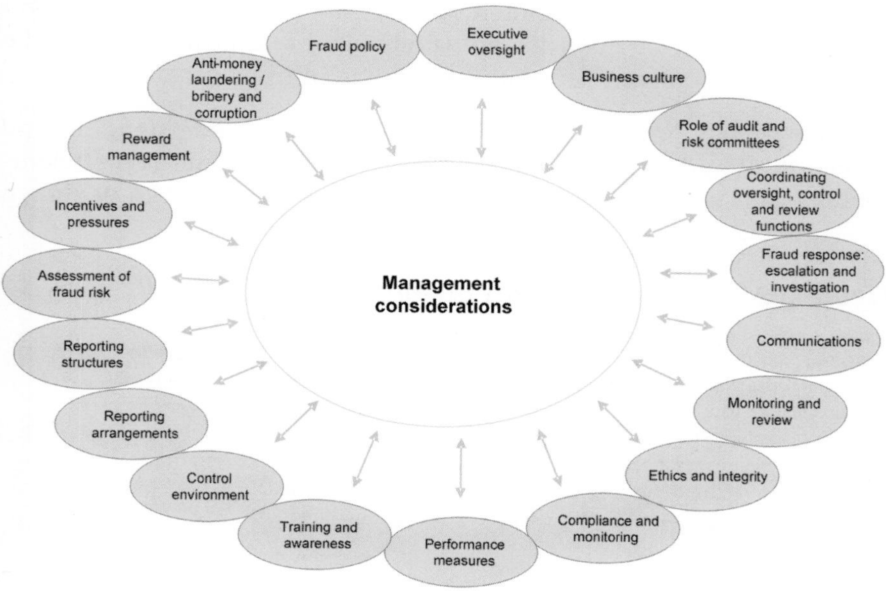

2.1 Causes of fraud

2.1.1 The power of pressure

Pressure is so often the root cause of fraud: pressure to build share price, to prop up an ailing part of the business, to reach targets, to meet bonus thresholds, to keep one's job, to maintain that promotion path.

1. A managing director increases his profits forecast to boost an apparent growth trend immediately prior to a proposed acquisition.

2. A management team realises that they are not going to meet their earn-out targets and manipulate period-end sales so that 'profits' can be brought forward to the current year.

3. The chairman and finance director of a company inflate its worth to raise equity and loan finance.

Such motives do not excuse fraud and in any event many pressures just have to be lived with. But it should not be a surprise when intense situations where people have a lot at stake lead to them breaking the rules. A look at court and press reports from the 1970s to today confirm that hard times bring things to boiling point.

Many businesses create essentially artificial pressures which over time result in an environment where fraud can flourish. Management are unwittingly incentivising staff to focus obsessively on narrow self-interest at the expense of the company. Internal controls get marginalised as a culture of immediate 'results' sets in. The rational assumption that pressure can be good for both individual and business has to be balanced by a common-sense understanding of human nature.

Accepting these uncomfortable facts is a key to understanding and preventing fraud. Business leaders and managers should focus relentlessly on this issue and continually ask themselves the questions shown in Figure 2.2.

Figure 2.2 Gauging pressures on employees

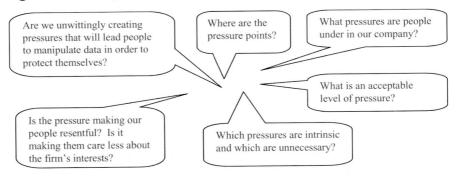

Answering these questions should result in a better understanding of risks to the business, allowing development of mitigating counter-measures together with early warning should high pressures result in inappropriate behaviour.

PRESSURE TO SHOW BETTER RESULTS

Following a communication from the groups CEO to ensure they met targets, senior management at a subsidiary company colluded to inflate year end value for total sales.

Tough business conditions meant the subsidiary was not going to meet target sales, so its management instructed finance staff to process a number of fictitious sales using existing customer names. The fraud was uncovered when new management at group initiated a review of the subsidiary.

2.1.2   Fragmentation of financial control

Today's businesses are moulded by a set of interlocking trends, all of which have their roots in improved technology and the faster communications that flow from it. The impact of this is considered in chapter 5 on IT fraud and abuse. The main issue is that internal controls and culture have not only failed to keep pace with the near revolution in business that has occurred since the 1980s, in some ways they have gone backwards.

Control, cash management and contracts are being managed throughout the business rather than centrally. This is not bad in itself, but it is all too often accompanied by a fragmentation of financial control and a dilution of the skills required to manage fraud. It has been a costly mistake which goes some way to explaining much of the explosion in fraud.

2.1.3   Empowerment

Business units now tend to have greater autonomy and higher penalties for failure as well as potentially higher rewards. Risk management and control need to take different forms in an empowered environment compared to a hierarchical one. Empowered units must acquire new skills and it is imperative that those monitoring branch offices and subsidiaries become more alert to early signs of fraud.

Control, cash management and similar activities are now often allocated to non-finance staff, eg a salesperson may be required to negotiate payment terms and manage credit risk. As a result business managers need a much more detailed understanding of financial controls along with the ability to identify and assess new risks. Yet many companies underestimate the training required to develop the necessary skills. Group management can also be reluctant to question business unit results closely for fear of undermining confidence in the new structure. Corporate culture does not change overnight just because leaders say it must.

2.1.4   Matrix management

Pooling staff from different functions for specific projects is now a very common way of working. Many companies have also reorganised traditional 'silo-based' functions such as sales, purchasing, production and finance, around key elements of the value chain. A number of financial disasters have arisen from the confusion of responsibilities that can so easily arise in such situations, for instance between local and functional reporting lines.

Central purchasing and finance staff are often relocated and report primarily to local project managers, retaining only a 'dotted line' to the head of group purchasing or the finance director. The Board may think this link remains strong, unaware that the dynamics of internal control have changed fundamentally. After all, local heads will have much more influence in hiring and firing as well as setting 'pay and rations'. It can be very difficult for centrally based staff to assess whether business units are achieving value for money.

Though power to award contracts has been given to many units for the first time, specialised knowledge is not always transferred with it. While mainline purchasing departments often have well-developed controls, there may be few of these in business units. Purchasing staff in a project team can also come under more pressure. Colleagues from other disciplines may see controls as pointless or self-serving bureaucracy that undermines the profitability on which their bonuses depend.

The ignorance or impatience of business unit managers can undermine rigorous bid assessment. Purchasing staff need time to answer key questions. Are bidders colluding? Have they previously provided services under another name? Can they deliver on price and quality? Would they report a fraud which affected the purchaser?

The following case study illustrates how changes in the organisation of the purchasing function had huge and damaging implications.

Inside a Purchasing Matrix

LOSING CONTROL OVER PURCHASING

A large company had a central procurement department however individual business units tended to initiate and award contracts based on their individual needs.

The management of a number of these business units complained whenever central procurement became involved, often making comments like "... procurement doesn't understand our business" and over time the business units were given greater autonomy regards procurement.

A number of cost overruns prompted senior management at head office to initiate a review. This resulted in a number of findings such as that: the same parent company owned or controlled a number of the bidders bidding for the same contract; payments had been made when it was clear that goods had not been provided; contract initiators often awarded contracts and also approved payments; and payments and returns had been manipulated impacting period end management accounts.

2.1.5 Downsizing, delayering and outsourcing

Radical improvements in technology have removed whole layers of middle management and led to head offices and divisional structures being cut, eliminated or contracted out. Some companies have not recognised that shedding staff can create new fraud risks. Expertise is lost, often at middle management level where it was strongest, and in vital technical functions such as internal audit. A radical reallocation of responsibilities and the development of new skills is required among remaining staff.

Outsourcing requires close attention to the quality of the contractor's controls, including regular reviews by the client company. This is particularly important for the processing of personal and financial data as outsourcing has sometimes resulted in the theft or leak of confidential customer information, eg from call centres.

2.1.6 What about loyalty?

The changes described above have had many positive effects on business efficiency and profitability, but it is vital to recognise that they can also do serious damage to employee loyalties. Staff are naturally unsettled by upheavals and care must be taken that they do not grow fearful and resentful. An undercurrent of hostility to management not only serves as a breeding ground for fraud, it also makes controls far more difficult to implement. A weakening of central oversight requires greater care and attention to staff in project teams and business units because more depends on their awareness, vigilance and desire to ensure the best outcome for the business.

2.2   Weak ethics and negative cultures

Some say the acid test of any business behaviour is what the Board, shareholders and stakeholders would think if news of it appeared in the national press. It is right to be concerned about image, but this is a short-sighted view of corporate ethics. Putting appearances before substance is the very frame of mind that smooths the way for fraud.

In the long run (and often in the short run too) an organisation is judged by how it treats people. Corporate values express themselves in how a company deals with employees, customers, suppliers and others. Ethical attitudes are the main determinants of culture and a key to effective fraud prevention.

1.   An ethical culture promotes clarity about right and wrong and eradicates the uncertainties which help fraud to thrive.

2.   By renouncing unnecessary pressures on staff, management can reduce incentives to commit fraud.

3.   By operating fairly a company maximises staff loyalty and makes employees allies in fraud prevention.

Poor business ethics and negative corporate cultures breed fraud. Their key characteristics are as follows.

2.2.1   Bad examples by leaders and managers

Business culture, and therefore business ethics, is set by a company's leaders – the chairman, chief executive, directors, senior and line management. It is too often the case that some of these set bad examples, including over-claiming of expenses, demanding consistently unreasonable results, promoting standards they do not work by, and manipulating data. It is apparent that staff pay far more attention to what their bosses do than to what they say. Hypocrisy by those in senior roles creates resentment, breeds cynicism and undermines loyalty, all of which facilitate fraud.

2.2.2   Aggression as a management style

A more competitive environment (and no doubt more subtle changes in social attitudes) has given rise to a more aggressive breed of business leaders. Their hallmarks are quick decisions and reliance on simple measures of success. Such leaders are often uninterested in detailed financial information or assessing risks in a structured way, indeed taking account of downsides can be seen as 'negative'. They have a tendency to blame those who bring bad news and pressure staff to appear positive regardless of underlying facts. Such managers make staff reluctant to raise concerns over suspected fraud.

2.2.3   Pressure overdrive

Performance measures and targets are a necessary part of business life. But they can be pushed too far, becoming unrealistic and overly aggressive. As shown above, excessive pressures increase the risk of fraud as staff struggle to fulfil expectations. The fear created by unrealistic targets encourages staff to manipulate data or hold off recognising liabilities.

2.2.4   Excessive trust

Many disasters have occurred because companies have refused to consider the possibility that fraudsters can be found in their own ranks. So controls focus on external fraud risks but not internal ones; there is also a reluctance to accept that management and long-serving colleagues can present a greater risk than junior employees; and exceptions and excuses are made for senior people.

2.2.5   Excessive secrecy

There is a big difference between commercial confidentiality and a culture which places a premium on secrecy (often a result of rigorous 'need-to-know' policies). Fraud becomes easier in a non-transparent business environment. The typical fraudster does not allow anyone to see the full picture; carefully controls access to certain personnel; deals with certain accounts personally and outside the main system; and keeps people off his patch. Moreover excessive sensitivity about disclosure can prevent one part of a business from learning about incidents that have occurred elsewhere.

2.2.6   Ethical confusion

If management fails to draw and communicate clear ethical lines, staff become confused as to acceptable business behaviour. Hallmarks of ethical confusion are as follows.

1. Key ethical messages are not integrated into internal communications, implying that the corporate code is a public relations gesture rather than a serious attempt to raise standards.

2. Staff are given little or no guidance on ethical dilemmas they might face. This is a particular problem in ensuring the integrity of financial reporting and information.

3. No serious attempt is made to find out whether staff understand what is required of them. Some companies expect their employees to submit an annual return stating that they have read the latest update of the ethical code when most have not read the original version let alone the updates.

2.2.7 Conflicting cultures

Problems can occur where any group of staff is not assimilated into group culture. This is most likely to occur where a business unit is a joint venture or has been recently acquired, particularly if the management has been retained.

Overseas acquisitions can present a significant challenge. It is easy to assume that the parent company's ethos will be adopted at home and abroad, but the global marketplace is still a complex matrix of customs. Every organisation must drill down to the local operational level before it can truly appreciate the fraud risks that it may be running. As the financial sector has discovered, relatively small outposts can expose a business as a whole to potentially catastrophic risks.

2.3 Divorcing strategy from risk awareness

Corporate strategy has a major impact on fraud. Yet risk management plans are not always developed in conjunction with strategy, which therefore fails to recognise threats to both the organisation as a whole and its individual parts. This results in deep-seated weaknesses in the strategic management process, eg by encouraging personal and business unit agendas at the expense of focusing on key risks.

IGNORING THE DOWNSIDES

A company planned to cut its material costs by 40 per cent. This ambitious goal merited a single line in the group's strategy document and was mentioned in only a single business unit plan. No implementation plan was prepared and no consideration was given to the new risks that could arise from such a big initiative.

The Board should have seen that the target had major business risk implications. It required:

- rationalisation of the company's supplier base;
- renegotiation of many of its contracts;
- operational changes, eg in timing of deliveries and payment of invoices; and
- improved purchasing skills.

The outcome was disastrous. Not only was there little progress on cost-cutting, there was also a significant increase in fraud.

Driving to reduce input costs can create significant fraud risks.

1. The simultaneous retendering and renegotiation of contracts increases the risk of purchasing frauds such as bid rigging, bid fixing and kickbacks.

2. New contracts involve discounts and rebates with potential for off-the-books arrangements. Rebates can be taken to profit conditional on assured future levels of business with the supplier.

3. Inadequate negotiating skills make a company more vulnerable to manipulation by suppliers, eg the latter acquire better payment terms to 'compensate' them for bogus upfront prices submitted purely to win the bid.

A lack of defined strategic objectives also leads to business units defining their own direction which can in turn expose the company to greater risks, eg purchasing fraud where a supplier supplies various business units and in collusion with a number of the company's staff, inflates price and quantity. Lack of a corporate-wide purchasing strategy means that independent review, which should pick up these types of discrepancies, is unlikely.

Figure 2.3 Perceptions of strategic drift

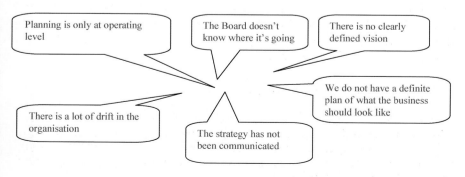

15

2.4   Impacts of organisational structure

Structural risk is perhaps the least understood aspect of the business environment, yet organisational structures are nevertheless the foundation of internal control. They define the roles, responsibilities and reporting lines on which controls are based and can undermine them too. All structures carry risk and the key is to understand those inherent in any particular arrangement.

The following case study shows how complex structures can create abnormal risk.

LACK OF COLLECTIVE RESPONSIBILITY

A board director and head of division (known as 'Z' here) in an overseas multinational understated annual forecast revenue from some remote locations by US$100 million. He then overstated the funding needed for certain projects by a similar amount.

The manipulation grew gradually over two years. Z's division always appeared to be exceeding its forecast (which had been understated) while spending less on the identified projects.

The end result was a US$200 million fraud, made possible by a number of structural issues which are outlined below.

How complex structures helped Z commit a major fraud

Figure 2.4 Simplified organisational structure in case study

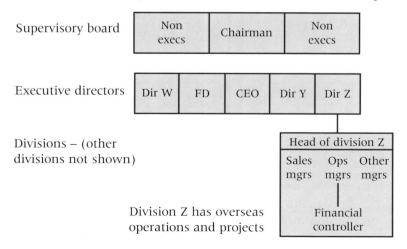

1. The executive directors seldom shared information about their divisions. Longstanding special arrangements meant Z's division did not report to group finance in the normal way.

2. The chief executive lacked authority over the other directors, Z in particular. The non-executive chairman dealt directly with management who still saw him in an executive role. Such a situation can only undermine legitimate authority.

3. Dominant personalities on a board can warp decision making. In this case director Z was good at keeping people off his patch.

4. An extreme divisional 'need-to-know culture' was imposed by Z. Many things were only known to him, and staff received little information on strategy and business objectives.

5. A low-status finance department finds it hard to manage fraud risks. In this case finance had relatively low status and Z's financial controller was in the third tier of management rather than being on the divisional board. His staff were relegated to 'bean counting'.

6. Uninvolved non-executive directors are of little value. The group's supervisory board structure aggravated their disconnection from the business. Though some non-executive directors were of a high calibre, structural problems made it difficult for them to obtain knowledge and exercise their powers effectively.

Sections **2.4.1** to **2.4.12** outline some of the issues where operational structure has not been clearly defined.

2.4.1 Blurred role definition

Clear roles and accountabilities are fundamental to fraud risk management and blurred lines undermine the best controls. Reviews can fail to pick these up if they focus on the mere presence of controls rather than their relationship with management structures.

Examples of such situations arise when a management structure has developed piecemeal and become a patchwork of reporting lines and historical anomalies; when there are unnecessary reporting levels; where managers have more than one 'hat' and such compound roles are not understood by everyone in the structure.

A reliable way of identifying disparities between a firm's actual and documented structure is to show the official organisation chart to staff. They often laugh and offer to draw what they see as the 'real' setup. Three or four conflicting versions may emerge, none of them reflecting the actual distribution of power.

Such confusion can have serious business implications.

1. People do not receive the right information at the right time. As a result, management may not pick up on unusual trends that provide the first clues to fraud.

2. Segregation of duties is compromised as staff feel obliged to work around meaningless structures.

3. There is a fragmentation of skills and functions. For instance, in a leasing company, skills which would normally be brought together in a portfolio management department were split between finance, customer services, etc., resulting in sub-optimal management of the lease portfolio.

4. Vague accountabilities make it difficult to apply effective performance measures.

5. Appropriate supervision is either not in place or is ineffective, leaving managers uncertain about actual reporting lines and unclear about which parts of the business they are responsible for.

2.4.2   Finance as 'the poor relation'

A low-status finance department has little power to deter fraud. Unless it has respect and support from the leaders of a business, other functions will seek greater independence and develop their own, less rigorous, practices, eg individual business units can end up determining revenue and cost revenue recognition differently. Controls become fragmented and ineffective, a perfect environment for a fraudster.

Figure 2.5 Signs of a weak finance department

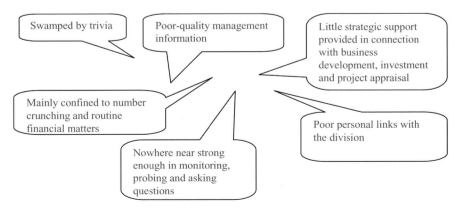

2.4.3 The perils of matrix management

Problems with matrix structures have underlain many frauds. They are not inherently risky, but they do involve different types of risk which companies sometimes fail to recognise.

2.4.4 Localised loyalties

A matrix management structure can facilitate loyalty to a country or local head rather than to a division or group. Pay and conditions may be determined by local rather than functional heads, as may hire-and-fire decisions. This leads to conflicts of loyalties and the creation of reporting lines unrecognised on official charts and unnoted in personnel files.

2.4.5 Special reporting arrangements

Units or individuals may be allowed special reporting arrangements outside the normal management structure. The reasons may be historic, eg the managing director of a newly purchased subsidiary was allowed originally to report directly to the group MD. An entity may be 'the chief executive's baby', with him denying real access to other senior managers. Local management are told they need not introduce group control systems provided they continue to meet budget. A manager is seen as a 'star' or 'difficult' and allowed to operate outside the usual rules. All such arrangements undermine proper controls.

2.4.6 Inadequate expertise

Local entities may not have the systems or skills to work the new matrix structure effectively and may be seen as too small to warrant spending money on improving matters. Yet new structures may need new skills and these should be in place before changes occur. There are no 'parallel runs' as is usually the case when starting a new computer system.

2.4.7 Structures versus risk-management procedures

New reporting lines can stop central management implementing and monitoring risk-management processes. Such arrangements can lead to situations where local managers fillet information before passing it to group level. This is a particular temptation when their units are faced with closure or disposal.

2.4.8   Inflated front-office status

Front-office functions can attract excessive applause. The resulting 'front-office heroes' culture can weaken controls and downgrade the importance of less glamorous roles. In some large brand-driven groups, advertising and marketing are lionised and allowed to ignore controls policed by low-status finance departments. One marketing department had few written contracts with suppliers and priced on an unclear basis without competitive tendering. Prices themselves were often agreed only after work had been completed. There were very close relationships with suppliers and lavish entertaining. Finance had no oversight of the department.

2.4.9   Marginalised business units

A matrix structure can leave business units marginalised during strategic decision making. As a result their functions may be compromised, eg by reduction and delayering which prevents them operating as originally envisaged.

2.4.10   Conflicting objectives

Conflicts may arise between customer-facing business units and centralised functions. The former may ignore group purchasing guidelines and expose themselves to fraud risks. They can also lose a sense of loyalty to the group as a whole. For example, buyers in one business unit may not liaise effectively with others in order to maximise group purchasing power.

2.4.11   Management structure undermined by reward structure

Disparities in pay levels can result in significant differences in competencies between departments, as well as resentment and poor morale.

2.4.12   Summary

These examples show that matrix structures can have unforeseen impacts. The lesson is simple. It is essential to analyse the risks inherent in a new organisational structure before it is established. Failure to do so exposes the business to a potentially immense increase in fraud risk.

2.5 Rewards as perverse incentives

Reward structures can sometimes subvert good controls by effectively introducing incentives to break the rules. This section examines how bonuses, earn-outs and other aspects of reward arrangements can contribute to the growth of fraud.

2.5.1 Bonuses

Too few companies make the connection between performance-based pay and internal control. Bank internal audit departments often have no data about reward structures for dealers and therefore find it difficult to assess dealing-room risks. Yet studying reward structures and dealing patterns together can reveal danger signs.

DONE DEALS

Sales staff in a leasing business were incentivised with reward packages which created immense pressure to close deals. Situations arose where they become aware of crucial information about a new or existing creditor. Rather than sharing this with the head of credit they suppressed the news until it was too late for the company to withdraw from the deal.

2.5.2 Earn-outs

Earn-outs are easily manipulated if controls focus on arithmetical accuracy rather than how inputs have been arrived at.

BOGUS TRANSACTION

A management team realised that a delayed contract would prevent them hitting their earn-out targets. So they created a fictitious customer, contract and suppliers, manipulating cash flows so they could bring forward the 'profit' into the current year and reach their targets.

2.5.3 Disparate pay levels

Disparities in relative pay levels can undermine controls, as the following example shows.

MONKEYS

ABC Limited had a large disparity in pay levels relative to market between technical and purchasing staff. The former were bright graduates paid significantly above market rates. Those in purchasing generally had low skill sets and were paid below market rates.

Purchasing was seen as a 'dumping ground'. Technical and other departments saw its staff as mere 'order placers' and sometimes jeered at them as 'monkeys'.

Purchasing had weak relationships with suppliers, rarely visiting their premises, and was often in a weak position due to poor negotiating skills. Technical developed its own extensive contacts with companies who went on to become 'chosen' suppliers despite there being equally well-qualified competitors.

Though formal tender procedures were usually followed, specifications were sometimes based on the chosen supplier's product. There was also an understanding with Technical that the supplier would win a contract even if its price was higher. Other parts of the business were not informed of this, and unfavoured suppliers were eliminated with a one- or two-line memo. The Technical department had effectively ousted Purchasing from the selection process.

2.6 Inadequate fraud risk management

It is now time to examine how weaknesses in risk management enables fraud to occur. Many companies have made the mistake of introducing more and more controls rather than developing more effective ones.

2.6.1 Low risk alertness

Fraud awareness is often very low or over-focused on certain types of risk, so creating significant blind spots.

Figure 2.6 *Signs of low fraud awareness*

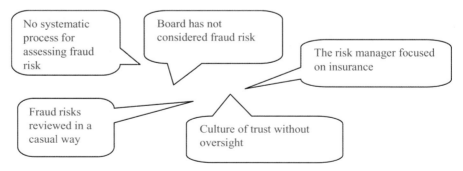

Problems include:

1. No systematic process for assessing fraud risk.

2. No forum or management time (such as a periodic Board agenda item) allocated to assessing fraud risk.

3. A focus on external and more visible frauds when management or experienced staff are best placed to manipulate accounts.

4. A lack of interest in common types of fraud, eg purchasing, travel, expenses or marketing.

5. A false perception that others were carrying out checks or reviews. It is often assumed that the risk-management function will identify fraud dangers despite being focused on insurance, health and safety, and business continuity planning.

A fraud awareness programme is an effective way of launching a number of related initiatives on ethics, risk management and control. This is considered further in **chapter 10**.

2.6.2 Failure to share and compare risk assessments

Risk reporting is often seen as a business unit responsibility with the group aggregating their assessments to establish 'interdependencies and accumulations' of risk. In fact it is vital for each main level of the business – group, business unit, department and project team – to carry out its own risk assessments and share and compare them to create a holistic picture.

Many issues might change a fraud risk profile.

1. Entry into new overseas markets with new distribution channels, agencies and intermediaries.

2. Joint-venture partners who may be involved in irregular business dealings.

3. Outsourcing and empowerment of business units spreading buying power to larger numbers of staff.

4. New accounting and payment systems creating unnoticed gaps in the handling of electronic payments.

5. Changes in reward structures increasing the risk of accounts manipulation.

6. Change in management and focus of the businesses objectives and direction.

2.6.3 Weak anti-fraud strategies

Many companies do not have an anti-fraud strategy. Others have one which only covers certain risks, eg an insurance company may focus on claimant fraud but overlook miss-selling on the underwriting side. This subject is covered in greater detail in **chapter 10**. Table 2.1 shows some typical areas of weakness.

Table 2.1 Typical missing elements of fraud risk management

In place	Missing
Business strategies at group and business unit level	No linking of fraud risk analysis to group or business unit strategies
Values charter	Integrity not listed as a value. Fraud issue generally excluded
Group risk-management manual	Out of date and gathering dust. Not launched effectively or integrated with the management calendar. No fraud risk profiling or recording in a risk register
Code of ethics	Annual sign off but messages not built into team briefings. No forum for staff to discuss ethical dilemmas
Fraud policy and response	Unknown to most staff. Buries key issues deep in text. No clear escalation and response process
Clear reporting channels	Fraud reporting channels not clearly defined. This may result in staff not raising suspicions of fraud, eg no provision for discussing concerns in confidence
Group accounting manual	Covers 'bean counting' and accounting policy issues but does not address fraud risk
Group and business risk	Models do not cover fraud risk specifically
Performance measures	Provide few indicators of fraud and fail to relate fraud risk to underlying business activity
Risk assessment	Fails to challenge business processes and controls to identify potential fraud risks
Minimum control guidelines and procedures manuals	Not linked to an assessment of fraud risk so difficult to assess whether all risks are covered
Corporate governance manual	Complex and hard to navigate with little coverage of fraud risk

2.7 Applying the lessons: four detailed case studies

2.7.1 Make or break for Mr Brown

CASE STUDY 1

A British-based multinational decided to expand in South East Asia. Its Australian subsidiary appeared to have the right man for the region: its finance director John Brown, a man with 20 years' group experience.

Group told the Australian CEO that the South East Asia business would continue to be booked in his subsidiary, but that Brown must have a free hand in line with the policy of empowerment being introduced throughout the group.

Unfortunately, this policy backfired.

Brown fell in with corrupt local business practices, approving bribes for local officials in order to win contracts.

His response to empowerment was to do business at all costs, breaching limits and controls and exposing the company to significant financial and regulatory risk.

When told that Brown must have a free hand, the Australian CEO took the view that Group had taken responsibility for supervision. In fact Group assumed the Australian subsidiary was keeping Brown under control. Neither provided appropriate oversight, eg by requiring reviews by independent management or internal audit which would have detected the more basic breaches.

Figure 2.7 shows the problem areas and the relevant management considerations are dark blue.

There were two main fraud risk-management issues.

1. There was no fraud risk assessment. Given a strategy of expanding into emerging markets a serious study by the board and senior management would have paid enormous dividends. Business risks relating to markets and distribution channels were assessed but wider issues went unrecognised.

2. There was no effective monitoring. Neither head office nor Australian senior management ensured independent review, including testing and interviews, to ensure compliance with company policy:

    (a) the matrix management structure created confusion over who was responsible for monitoring Brown. The result was that no one did, and

Figure 2.7 Problem areas in case study 1

(b) many of the controls that management thought it had over their newly empowered staff proved entirely ineffective. Empowerment requires more rigorous controls, not less. Corporate culture does not change merely because senior managers say it must.

Wider business issues were also relevant. They include:

1. The company's culture was trusting of longstanding colleagues. Brown's bosses were prepared to approve his transactions without seeking any serious rationale.

2. There were important problems with reward structures and performance measures. The unspoken message was that if Brown succeeded he was bound for senior management, but that failure would kill any future advancement. It was make or break.

3. Local culture played a part. Brown was operating in a country with a different language, very few local professionals and considerable corruption amongst the officials he was dealing with.

2.7.2   Who wants to be a millionaire?

CASE STUDY 2

Wanting to impress her new beau, a finance manager in the subsidiary of a leading company defrauded £1.2 million from a division with a £30 million turnover. She started by stealing £15,000, building up to a payment of over £500,000.

She gained access to payment data, falsified details and used authentication devices and passwords to transmit payment instructions. The thefts were hidden by manipulating reconciliations (which she prepared) and concealing the amounts in poorly controlled areas of both the profit and loss account and balance sheet. The crime might not have been discovered had it not been for a review of the business's accounting records when the finance manager had taken a few days off.

Figure 2.8 Problem areas in case study 2

Some of the relevant factors relate to fraud risk management, others relate to the wider business environment. It is crucial to understand the link between the two.

In the above case study the fraud risk management issues were as follows.

1. Controls were more apparent than real. Electronic authentication devices were used, but segregated password control went

unenforced. The finance manager completed reconciliations and concealed the fraudulent payments by changing payment details or misrepresenting payment requests to management.

2. Weaknesses in performance measures enabled the fraud to be concealed. Budgets were not monitored closely and the fraudster hid debits in various creditor accounts, taking advantage of confusion over who had ultimate responsibility for them.

3. There was no assessment of fraud risks in the payments process.

4. Fraud awareness was low. Despite many warning signs (the fraudster purchased a number of cars and began to enjoy a lavish lifestyle), her behaviour was not considered suspicious.

5. There was no overall anti-fraud strategy.

There were also wider business environment issues.

1. People factors were important with low fraud awareness among management and staff and no training to highlight critical controls.

2. Management structure played a part. The company had moved from a hierarchical to an empowered structure without upgrading its controls. Virtually all finance responsibilities had been devolved to the business. The fraud could have been spotted easily if greater attention had been paid to individual payments and their supporting documentation.

2.7.3   Saving for a rainy day

This case study involves both accounts manipulation and purchasing fraud. The former provides the perfect cover for the latter. It also involved internal and external collusion.

CASE STUDY 3

Marketing managers in the UK subsidiary of an overseas multinational stole £5 million through a variety of purchasing frauds. Rather than report that expenditure was significantly below budget, they hung on to the surplus by accruing actual savings to meet budget in the monthly management accounts, putting through forward purchase orders, and entering into collusive pre-invoicing with suppliers around the year end.

The marketing managers initially wanted to use the surplus as a hedge against years when their budget might be cut. But their manipulation provided cover for collusive over-billing by suppliers together with personal profit from kickbacks and bogus invoices from suppliers in which managers had a financial interest.

The company had grown significantly with turnover increasing by a factor of ten. The goal had been to increase market share aggressively, so 'units sold' became the key measure of performance. Sales revenue came next and bottom-line profit was relegated to third place.

Downward pressure on costs fell off as the budget for advertising, marketing and promotion was based simply on a percentage of budgeted sales. There was no development on the basis of strategic need or specific campaigns. It was made clear that questions would only be asked if the budget was exceeded and the actual spend was significantly below this level.

Figure 2.9 Problem areas in case study 3

Fraud risk-management problems were as follows.

1. A key performance measure, the budget/actual comparison, was undermined. Actual figures were accrued to the budgeted level by putting through accruals in the monthly management accounts. Forward purchase orders were put through in place of the accruals at year end and monitoring was ineffective.

2. Risk assessment was weak. Given the company's strategy, it was important for senior management at both group and business unit levels to assess the risks inherent in aggressively building market share.

In terms of business environment culture played an important part. Sales and marketing managers were corporate 'heroes' and the Board did not want to question them closely on how they were spending the company's money as long as they stayed within budget.

The following set of linked questions and checks would have quickly uncovered the manipulation.

1. Where are the pressures in the profit and loss account? Rank them. This would have highlighted the poor focus on cost levels.

2. How is the budget set? What is the linkage between budgets and underlying events campaigns and initiatives? This would have identified slack in the budget.

3. Does the company accrue actual to budget in the monthly management accounts? This would have revealed the first signs of manipulation.

4. If so, ask what happens at the year end. Check the year-end period for forward purchase orders.

5. Forward purchase orders usually indicate collusive pre-invoicing. Check out invoices near the year end; this will reveal manipulation of budget and actual figures.

Where there is collusive pre-invoicing there are likely to be other irregularities on the relevant supplier account – for example no contract, no competitive tendering, no clear basis for pricing, poor documentation, prices agreed informally after work completed, lavish entertaining, etc. Where these problems exist it is likely that there will be some form of purchasing fraud.

2.7.4 The £20 million 'black hole'

The fourth case is a classic accounts manipulation fraud.

CASE STUDY 4

A financial controller had to examine stock differences. Faced with the demands of a year-end audit he decided to raise some false sales invoices on dormant sub-accounts to cover up the problem. Regarded as a high flyer, he had no desire to attract increased scrutiny from head office. He intended to reverse the invoices and look into the stock differences once the auditors had signed off.

In fact he moved on to manipulating poorly controlled inter-company accounts and smoothed various revenue and expense captions in the profit and loss account to make results appear in line with budget. After three years what appeared to be a £10 million profit actually concealed a £10 million loss.

3 Understanding white-collar fraudsters

Corporate fraud is about exploiting organisational weaknesses but it is perpetrated by individuals. The more aware we are of what motivates 'insider' fraudsters, and their key characteristics, the better equipped we will be to stop them.

3.1 Why do they do it?

Motive, opportunity and rationalisation make up the well-known 'fraud triangle'.

1. People commit fraud when a motive coincides with an opportunity and the potential reward outweighs the risks. Motivations can be personal (such as the desire for a lavish lifestyle) or business related (wanting to meet or exceed targets).

2. The opportunity may arise because there is no perceived deterrent. It is linked to the extent and effectiveness of controls aimed at preventing and detecting fraud.

3. Rationalisation is the fraudster's internal dialogue that provides him with a 'justification' for the crime, eg an individual determines that he is 'owed' or deserves additional income at the expense of the company.

Motive + Opportunity + Rationalisation = Fraud.

Those who can rationalise selfish gain (because of pressure and/or greed) commit fraud if allowed to do so.

It is worth exploring motivation and rationalisation in more detail. There are three basic categories.

3.1.1 Work and personal pressures

We have seen how pressure is often the root cause of fraud: to reach targets, to keep one's job, to maintain a promotion path, to prop up an ailing part of the business. The examples in section 2.1.1 are again set out below.

Figure 3.1 Fraud triangle

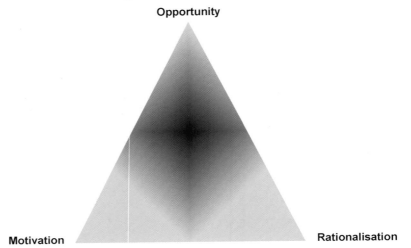

1. A managing director increases his profit forecast to boost the apparent growth trend immediately prior to a proposed acquisition.

2. A management team realises they are not going to meet their earn-out targets and manipulate cash flows so that 'profits' can be brought forward to the current year.

3. The chairman and finance director of a company inflate the company's worth to raise equity and loan finance.

In addition, there are also personal pressures, some more understandable than others: shortage of money for essential bills, serious gambling habits, expensive divorce settlements and extravagant lifestyles, pressure from spouses or mistresses. A recession often results in a higher level of fraud, particularly if it coincides with unusually high levels of personal debt.

3.1.2 Greed and egotism

Though some fraudsters are driven by intense objective pressures, stealing to keep a mistress or a house with a swimming pool should be categorised as greed rather than need. The *Oxford English Dictionary* defines greed as 'intense or excessive desire'. It is a hunger that breaks the bounds of decency or reason.

We see this in the many cases of already well-off people who want to 'skim something off the top'. It is far from uncommon, for instance, to find directors 'fiddling' expense claims. KPMG Forensic's 2007 *Profile of a Fraudster*, which examined 360 actual cases of corporate fraud throughout Europe, South Africa and India, found that no less than 47 per cent of corporate fraudsters admitted that greed was their principal driver. Given the natural tendency to hide a shameful motive, it is safe to assume that the real proportion is higher.

Greed is closely associated with egotism, an obsession with self that disregards the rights and needs of others. Some fraudsters have been described as having a 'superiority complex'. One manifestation of this is 'wanting to outwit the system'.

1. A highly paid operations manager in a London bank fiddled his expense claims because it gratified him to break the rules. Unfortunately the urge to boost his self-esteem morphed into outright greed and he moved onto kickbacks from suppliers in the form of cash, holidays and payment of school fees.

2. A fraudster who had been released from prison went on to defraud banks of £1 million. He did not smoke, drink, gamble or own a car, despite having ten driving licences. He created nine different identities with 11 banks and opened 90 accounts. Each identity was documented by his taking a new driving test in order to obtain a licence. He had a sophisticated card index system, with every identity fully referenced and different colours marking each bank account. The police called him the 'pipe and slippers fraudster' so mundane was his life apart from crime.

3.1.3 'Entitlement' and revenge

Fraudsters often use a real or manufactured sense of injustice to rationalise their crimes. Two examples illustrate this.

1. A group of marketing managers believed they were poorly compensated for their contribution to the UK business and found ways to cream off an additional 'bonus' rather than repatriate profits to the overseas head office.

2. A Swiss bank paid commission to another institution for introducing clients. The directors who had arranged the introductions believed that they, not the institution, should benefit from the commissions and had them paid into their personal accounts.

A desire for revenge is a sub-set of this feeling of 'entitlement'. Someone may feel exploited, ill-treated, denied the pay or position that he needs or is entitled to. Organisations with low morale (arising from, say, a redundancy programme or high levels of unnecessary drudgery) are particularly vulnerable.

3.2 Profiling the fraudster

What sort of person commits fraud? At first glance, an average fraudster is not much different from an average person. Yet there are powerful and persistent patterns amongst significant white-collar criminals. The above survey (profile of a fraudster – refer to section 3.1.2) of corporate or white-collar fraudsters provides a number of important findings such as the corporate fraudster:

1. is usually an insider: 89 per cent of the sample were employees.

2. tends to be a manager: 60 per cent of the total were senior managers (including board members). Over four-fifths of cases were at managerial level.

3. tends not to be suspected: 55 per cent had not fallen under prior suspicion (that 45 per cent *had* clearly underlines the benefits of effective detection mechanisms).

4. exploits organisational and personal weakness: 49 per cent took advantage of weak internal controls and 15 per cent colluded with others.

5. is usually a serial offender: 65 per cent committed ten or more frauds and 32 per cent 50 or more.

Figure 3.2 Quantity of fraudulent acts/transactions

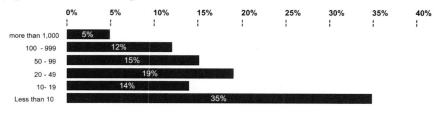

6. usually has access to sensitive data: 36 per cent worked in finance, 32 per cent in operations/sales, 11 per cent were CEOs and 9 per cent were in procurement. External fraudsters tended to be suppliers, customers and subcontractors.

7. tends to work alone: the perpetrator acted independently in over two-thirds of cases. Groups of five or more were uncommon.

8. tends to be a long-serving employee: over 50 per cent had been employed with the defrauded business for at least six years. Only 13 per cent of cases involved staff who had been with the company for less than two years.

4 Common indicators and risk factors

It is now time to highlight common fraud indicators and risk factors. Bear in mind that while we can group fraud into three broad types – theft, corruption and accounts manipulation – they can fall into more than one type, such as in the case of 'counterparty' which also could be grouped under heading of corruption. Table 4.1 sets out their variations.

Table 4.1 What risks does an organisation face?

Risk 1 – Theft	Risk 2 – Corruption	Risk 3 – Accounts manipulation
Procurement – the organisation may be a victim of collusion resulting in an inflated price for a contract	**Self-dealing** – an official steals funds for personal use	**Revenue recognition** – amounts are usually booked in advance of when they can be properly recognised
Counterparty – the organisation may be transacting with fictitious counterparties, or with counterparties related to employees or directors	**Bribery** – payments to, and acceptance of, bribes by public officials in return for preferential treatment (eg to avoid tax or to obtain public benefit)	**Purchases** – costs are usually deferred and not recognised in the correct period
Misappropriation – this applies to tangible assets (cash, stock, other materials) and intangible assets (intellectual property, sensitive data taken by a departing employee)	**Procurement** – the organisation makes payments to obtain contracts or concessions	**Inventory** – the value of inventory is usually understated, to increase profits achieved in the accounting period
Identity theft – this applies equally to organisations as it does to individuals. An organisation's identity can be used by a third party fraudulently to obtain goods, services or credit	**Organised crime** – the organisation's funds or employees are involved in organised and illegal business concerns (drugs or arms trafficking, money laundering, etc.)	**Cash** – this is manipulated so that it appears that an organisation has more cash than it in fact does, usually to preserve finance lines
IT fraud – systems could be subject to infiltration by hackers, could be bombarded by 'spam', or could be used in phishing claims		
Expense fraud – employees submit fraudulent expense claims		

All three are the result of the crystallisation of certain organisational weakness and are marked by various warning signs.

4.1 Management level

4.1.1 Autocratic style

The dominance of a chairman, chief executive or function head has been a major factor in many frauds. There should be particular concern in the following cases.

1. Senior management are frequently overruled by a chairman or chief executive.

2. There is no meaningful board-level debate.

3. One director has exclusive control over a significant part of the business with little or no independent review by senior colleagues.

4. Only one or two directors are aware of key transactions.

4.1.2 No clear and positive corporate ethics

This leads to a proliferation of 'grey areas' covering expenses, entertainment, gifts, commissions and conflicts of interest. The resulting indifference and uncertainty creates endless opportunities for fraudsters.

4.1.3 'Results at any cost' mentality

Setting goals is an essential management tool, but senior management may become so concerned to hit targets that they have little interest in other responsibilities. It is then a short step to manipulating results. Companies take their character from the top and when senior people cut corners it encourages a similar approach to financial controls throughout the organisation.

4.1.4 Lax attitudes to legal requirements

This should arouse suspicion. Indifference to the law on matters such as directors' interests or dealers' attitudes to counterparty limits say something important about the culture of a business, its control environment and the integrity of those running it.

4.1.5 Poorly defined business strategy

This helps to mould an environment in which fraud thrives. Symptoms include low morale, high staff turnover and an undue emphasis on short-term targets.

4.2 Staff level

4.2.1 Poor quality

Internal controls can only be as good as the people operating them so a company's inability to attract high-calibre personnel indicates serious problems.

4.2.2 Low morale

This means staff are less likely to operate controls effectively. Some may also want to avenge themselves on the company, particularly when faced by redundancy or unit closure.

4.2.3 High staff turnover

This may indicate unhappiness at how a business is run, oppressive working conditions or disquiet about the activities of senior managers.

4.2.4 Unquestioning obedience

This is expressed in passivity, lack of initiative, fear and unwillingness to ask questions and indicates that staff are likely to acquiesce or collude in fraud by their superiors.

4.2.5 Skills gaps

This can affect the ability of staff to manage fraud risk. A purchasing department will be put in a weak negotiating position and be more vulnerable to supplier manipulation of the bid process.

4.3 Organisation and structure

4.3.1 Ambiguous attitudes to control

These may derive from lack of commitment by directors or senior management, or an over-emphasis on short-term financial targets. They show up in attempts to restrict the scope of audit and inspection work, and access to individuals or documents.

4.3.2 Shadow hierarchies

Some organisations display marked differences between formal and actual hierarchies. Forceful personalities exert authority and influence disproportionate to their status. They acquire power to override controls and suppress information, conditions essential to the concealment of fraud. For instance, a head of department sees himself as the driving force behind the business and behaves as an owner rather than manager.

Nepotism is still a very real problem in many companies and this also undermines the official chain of command. In one company the deputy head of procurement was the son-in-law of the board director to whom the procurement chief reported.

Figure 4.1 The shadow hierarchy

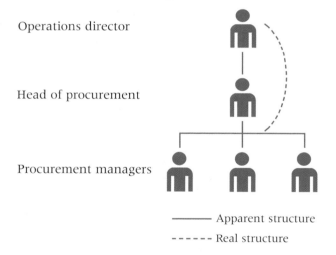

Operations director

Head of procurement

Procurement managers

——————— Apparent structure

- - - - - - Real structure

4.3.3 Obsessive secrecy

A High Court judge once described secrecy as the 'badge of fraud'. Particular attention should be paid to the following situations.

1. Information is provided only after repeated requests.

2. A transaction's true nature becomes clear only after examining many individual pieces of information.

3. Transactions and structures lack a clear business purpose.

'MY DOOR IS ALWAYS CLOSED'

It was one thing for the finance director to be the only senior manager to keep his door shut. It was quite another when he had his office sound-proofed. Colleagues became suspicious and he was later charged with fraud.

4.3.4 Cronyism

This is an excessive reliance on relationships which undermines prudent safeguards. The following example outlines the dangers.

COSY SUPPLIER RELATIONSHIPS

An entire procurement department was hired from a competitor and given complete freedom to run a centralised purchasing function. It turned out that five members of the new team brought their old 'crony' suppliers with them. These companies always won contracts; either invitation letters to other companies were not sent (despite being put on the files), or the crony suppliers won on the basis of bids that were later invalidated by over-billing. The director of procurement even had shareholdings in two of the suppliers. If the company had checked a little further they would have discovered that the team's former employer had suffered a similar fraud at their hands.

4.3.5 Performance-linked compensation

This can create temptations both to commit and to turn a blind eye to fraud. Senior management may be reluctant to ask probing questions about the basis and quality of profits when staff appear to be making a great deal of money for the company. Yet the 'profits' may be based on unauthorised or bogus deals.

4.3.6 Complex structures

A number of major frauds involve the use of 'parallel' organisations. These are companies under the control of one or more directors or senior managers who are supposed to be working in the interests of the company they actually work for. In fact they use the parallel company to trade with the company that employs them. Even a suggestion of such structures should cause immediate concern unless the arrangements are transparent and well understood. Directors and auditors should be fully briefed on such companies and their relationship to the main organisation. It is essential that an effective conflict of interests policy is in place and that this activity is monitored and enforced.

4.3.7 Weak supervision of remote locations

Fraud is most likely to occur where supervision and control is least effective. Remote offices, warehouses and factories may need a high degree of autonomy, but this can be abused if they are not regularly monitored.

The same risk applies to activities regarded as peripheral to the main business, eg company car schemes, disposal of fixed assets and repair of goods under warranty. Problems may also occur in relation to newly acquired subsidiaries where management style or business culture differs markedly from that of the group as a whole.

4.3.8 Bad reputation

The views of other participants in the market usually provide useful insights into a company's products, people and way of doing business. The issues they identify may highlight a number of fraud-related weaknesses.

4.4 Financial arrangements

4.4.1 Accounting systems out of sync with business development

Rapid growth, major changes in methods and shifts to new business sectors can leave accounting systems struggling to keep up. This has been particularly so in banking which has seen rapid evolution in financial instruments and products. Similar problems have occurred when a swift succession of acquisitions makes a group outgrow its command structure.

4.4.2 Liquidity problems

A number of major frauds have been motivated by the need to meet regulatory obligations and thus report expected values or in order to give a more favourable impression of the business's financial soundness.

4.4.3 Profits well in excess of industry norms

Profits well in excess of industry norms usually merit close examination. They may indicate that the company has not recognised appropriate revenue or costs, or that they should be recognised in another (prior or future) period.

5   IT fraud and abuse

New technology, particularly Information Technology (IT), creates opportunities for fraud. Business is now heavily dependent on computing and the internet for operational, accounting and management information systems. Traditional controls over money, data and customer contact have been eroded by vastly increased data flows and systems that allow access to that data.

Reputational damage from IT fraud and abuse – such as attacks on online merchant websites or data theft – can easily exceed any immediate financial loss. A single disgruntled employee can steal and share confidential client information, disable a network and corrupt essential data. Risks are compounded by the sheer complexity of new technology, which tempts management to delegate security issues to technical staff and rely on 'off the peg' safeguards.

Yet risk management is as much the key to business protection in this area as it is in any other. Managers need to understand key risks and solutions if they are to allocate resources intelligently let alone approve, operate and analyse improved controls. What follows is written with the general manager in mind.

5.1   Providing advantage to the fraudster

IT has given fraudsters three significant advantages.

5.1.1   Access

The internet has removed many of the safeguards previously provided by physical boundaries. Frauds can now be committed without actually entering a company's premises, and even from another country. The open systems and networks which boost e-commerce further increase the risk of hacking and illegal access. Segregation of IT-related duties breaks down as improvements in hardware and software reduce the need for large numbers of support staff.

5.1.2   Empowerment

There has been immense growth in the processing power of PCs and mobile devices such as BlackBerries©, PDAs and smart phones.

Fraudsters can now store large amounts of data on small devices and thus either import or export information into or out from the company (although the technically literate fraudster usually does not need physical access). Hundreds of illicit websites also provide regularly updated information and software, which enables data manipulation usually for free.

5.1.3 Concealment

The routing of internet transactions through multiple servers, often in a number of countries, allows fraudsters to hide their identities and locations. The growth of wi-fi connections in public places now allows fraudsters to hack into systems 'on the move' rather than tying them to a fixed location. The ease with which funds can be transferred to different jurisdictions also makes recovery action more difficult.

5.2 How IT fraud occurs

There are three types of IT crime.

1. Computer-assisted fraud where IT is used to process or produce a fraudulent transaction.

2. Computer-generated fraud where IT is tampered with to produce a fraudulent result.

3. Computer abuse: any activity which corrupts or deletes software and the data it supports, or which interrupts data processing.

Fraudulent processing may take place at any of the three key stages in a computer transaction.

1. Input-related: computer-assisted fraud involving manipulation of data entries.

2. Program-related: computer-generated fraud consisting of unauthorised changes to programs or processing systems.

3. Output-related: manipulation or suppression of computer output.

Figure 5.1 provides a simplified overview of the main processes occurring in a typical computer system.

Figure 5.1 Typical computer processes and frauds

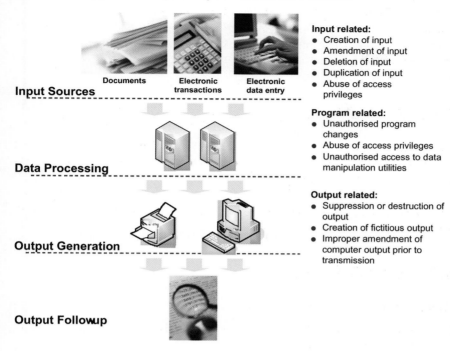

Input Sources

Documents   Electronic transactions   Electronic data entry

Data Processing

Output Generation

Output Followup

Input related:
- Creation of input
- Amendment of input
- Deletion of input
- Duplication of input
- Abuse of access privileges

Program related:
- Unauthorised program changes
- Abuse of access privileges
- Unauthorised access to data manipulation utilities

Output related:
- Suppression or destruction of output
- Creation of fictitious output
- Improper amendment of computer output prior to transmission

5.3   Input-related fraud

Input-related fraud is the most common of the three as it can be committed wherever data is amended or altered, even during system entry. It requires nothing more than understanding of relevant inputting procedure and the supporting clerical and approval processes. The various input-related frauds are set out below.

5.3.1   Creation of input

This can be as simple as inserting an additional expense requisition into an existing batch, or changing an employee's bank account payee details.

SHARED PASSWORD

An accounts clerk discovered the password of the second cheque signatory. This enabled him to make and 'authorise' a number of large payments to his personal account. The frauds were not picked up because no one checked bank confirmation documents properly.

5.3.2 Amendment of input

This involves changing data prior to inputting, eg padding an expense claim or changing the name and address of a loan applicant.

> **PERSONAL INTEREST**
>
> A data entry clerk reduced the interest rate on certain personal loan applications when entering them into the bank's computer. In return the applicants paid the clerk 50 per cent of the interest saved.

5.3.3 Deletion of input

Usually this occurs prior to entry and can be as simple as the removal of an item from a batch of records or the deletion of the entire batch.

5.3.4 Duplication of input

This involves re-processing information (such as a request for payment or stock shipment). It may involve submitting both the original document and a copy, or re-inputting the original during a later cycle.

5.3.5 Abuse of access privileges

Data can also be faked or altered by using facilities for correcting data that has been accidentally corrupted; this is a process which bypasses normal reporting procedures.

The more complex the system, the greater the need for reconciliation checks. Real-time or 'straight-through' processing reduces the opportunity for 'cut-offs' which enable balancing across all systems (though this type of processing requires sophisticated automated fraud detection systems). A surprising number of software packages provide no means of identifying transactions supposed to have failed part way through an update, despite this being a common disguise for input fraud.

It is important to distinguish between different types of input fraud as the associated risks can vary considerably and require different levels of control. The alteration of standing data input is usually more difficult to detect as the fraud entails a single act whereas changes to transaction data involve repeated interventions. Examples of standing data for an insurance company customer will include a correspondence address, bank account number(s) and beneficiary name(s). In that case 'transactional data' would refer to the payment method and the amount on the policy. A single act of fraud could include modification of the customer's address in order to divert account statements. Fraudulent diversion of claim payments would require recurring actions in order to make the request and secure authorisation.

Table 5.1 Examples of standing and transaction data frauds

Fraudulent procedure	Standing data examples	Transaction data examples
Creation of invalid output data	Creation of a bogus employee	Creation of a fictitious supplier invoice
Amendment of existing input data	Changes to a customer's discount percentage	Increasing the discount offered to a customer on a one-off order entry form
Deletion of valid input data	Deleting a valid notice of death of a registered shareholder to enable diversion of dividends	Deletion of slow response time records at a call centre to improve performance statistics
Duplication of valid input data	Duplication of new insurance policy details to inflate new business statistics	Duplication of an invoice for services where checks are not taken to confirm goods received

5.3.6 Warning signs

1. Poor segregation of computer-related duties and responsibilities.

2. Excessive levels of system access by clerical and supervisory staff (usually justified 'in case something goes wrong').

3. Sharing of passwords (which undermines user accountability).

4. Passwords still in use after individuals have left the company.

5. Processing problems which continually require attention from the same member of staff.

6. High levels of customer and supplier queries/complaints.

7. Accounts balanced only via extensive adjustments and specialist inputs.

8. Unusual transactions on reconciliation suspense reports.

9. Failures in trans-systems reconciliation checks, eg for integrated software packages where one input requires several transactions affecting a number of ledgers.

5.4 Program-related fraud

This involves illicit manipulation of computer programs or operations. It requires a thorough understanding of the information being processed and a sound knowledge of the systems involved.

It takes three forms:

- unauthorised program changes;
- abuse or circumvention of access privileges; or
- unauthorised access to data-processing utilities.

Examples include:

1. Tampering with a program so that it generates despatch documentation without an accompanying financial record.
2. Subtracting the 'rounding-off' value from each transaction and adding the money to a special account.
3. Changing programs so that sales commission is calculated by gross sales figures before credit notes are taken into account.

ROUNDING DIFFERENCES

A bank computer programmer inserted code into an interest calculation program which directed income from 'rounding down' into his own accounts. He stole £120,000 in four months.

An increasing number of end users are adept at designing and developing sophisticated spreadsheet and database applications. They tend to know much less about protecting their work from abuse. For instance, the spreadsheet or database application is often tested by running confidential data, which is then stolen because the user has forgotten to delete it. To make matters worse, proper access controls and audit trails often go unactivated, making it difficult to identify potential culprits.

5.4.1 Warning signs

1. Poor control over program changes.
2. Little or no user involvement in testing program changes. Operational users can help identify potential weaknesses.
3. High unexplained volume of program changes.
4. Absence of audit controls on program codes. Programmers can include malicious code to perform purportedly 'authorised' operations.
5. Poor controls over physical access to computer facilities.

5.5 Output-related fraud

Computer systems produce many types of output, from screen messages to hard-copy reports and cross-border electronic payment instructions. Output fraud requires detailed knowledge of how information moves within a system, together with understanding of the supporting clerical and approval processes (such as the identity of the person who receives exception reports, or which office printer generates pre-signed cheques).

Output-related fraud takes the following forms:

- suppression or destruction of output;

- creation of fictitious output; or

- improper amendment of computer output prior to transmission.

Examples include:

- suppressing entries which highlight non-performing loan customers;

- creating fictitious or duplicated insurance policies in support of inflated new business claims;

- amending payee details on Bankers Automated Clearing System (BACS) payment files; and

- theft of computer-generated cheques.

> **COVERING HIS TRACKS**
>
> A finance clerk with system access changed bank and payment details on payment electronic files which resulted in a number of payments going to the clerk's personal account. Management were not aware of these changes and authorised the payment based on paper document evidence.

5.5.1 Warning signs

1. Shared passwords.

2. Junior staff with unusually wide system access (usually justified as a precaution in case of illness or emergency).

3. Processing problems which continually require fixing by a particular member of staff whose work is hard to check.

4. Staff making unusual use of computer resources, eg accessing them out of hours.

5. Abnormal use of remote access (one credit controller in a betting company always allocated credit to his betting account on Saturdays from an offsite location).

6. Large volumes of items, or unusual transactions, in reconciliation or suspense accounts (common places for concealing frauds).

5.6   Internet fraud and disruption

Organisations are often surprised to find out how much can be learnt about them online. Examples include processes and procedures, manufacturing methods, research results, authorisation lists and holiday rosters. Many organisations invest heavily in security only to be compromised by basic errors. Once obtained, data can be quickly transmitted anywhere in the world.

5.7   The perfect environment for fraud

When asked why he robbed banks, American gunman Willie Sutton replied, 'Because that's where the money is'. Career criminals are moving into internet fraud for the same reason plus the added advantages of much easier access, near-anonymity and poor precautions. It is the perfect environment for fraud.

Internet-based fraud is increasingly dominated by organised crime which also has extensive links with freelance hackers. Both search continually for weaknesses in corporate procedures, systems and personnel (see **chapter 9**).

PLUNDERING THE TAXMAN

Britain's tax authority reported systematic attacks on its online self-assessment system with fraudsters filing bogus returns and claiming millions in 'repayments'. In one case 50 purported tax agents were used to make 14,000 false returns for a total of £34 million.

CAPTURING CARDS

A man was arrested after trying to sell an encrypted CD-ROM with details of 100,000 credit cards for US$260,000. He had captured the details by hacking into the computers of companies undertaking credit-card transactions.

ACCOUNT TAKEOVER

A group of rogue call-centre operators at an online gambling company stole customers' bank details and sold them on internet forums. The buyers then used the data to divert funds out of customer accounts. The company discovered the fraud via CCTV footage which showed operators noting down confidential information.

Political militants and even governments have discovered that IT attacks can do far more damage to companies than demonstrations, blockades or 'traditional' forms of criminal damage. A favoured method is a 'denial-of-service' attack (see **5.8.2**). They have also hacked into and altered company websites, replacing original messages with their own, sometimes pornographic, message and images. Extortionists use some of the same techniques, creating disruption in order to force an organisation to pay them off.

CHANGING THE IMAGE

An airline changed its name following a major plane crash. Its website was then hacked to show a picture of a burning plane and the caption 'So we killed a few people, big deal'.

5.8 Hackers

Hackers (also known as crackers, phreakers, and cyberpunks) break into computer systems. Some do it simply for the challenge, but since many advertise their successes and share software via specialist internet forums their techniques are copied by those with criminal intent. Gaps in an organisation's computer security can be posted on the internet within hours of discovery.

Once inside a system the hacker explores the access rights configuration and the layout of the system to find out which parts of the server he can access. He (it is often a man) can sometimes gain 'superuser' status, a credential allowing access to every function running on the server. 'Packet-sniffers' (also known as 'LAN analysers') are then planted to record any information transmitted over the network.

5.8.1 How hackers access a system

1. Spam e-mails are perhaps the easiest and most common way to plant a computer virus or to lure users onto a bogus website in order to obtain confidential information such as banking details.

2. 'Free' content and trojans. Internet users seeking free downloads are usually asked to install a piece of software such as an ActiveX component. Many of these are in fact disguised viruses called 'trojans' which e-mail out every piece of information they find, often leaving users unaware of what has happened. Users should only download content from authorised and/or legal sites.

3. War-dialling software systematically dials telephone numbers to find back-door access to corporate systems.

4. Cracker software works every conceivable password combination (using dictionaries and other common word, name and number lists) in order to enter a system.

5. Port scanners test each computer port (points where remote connections are made) looking for any which have been left open.

6. Social engineering mainly entails obtaining confidential information via deception, for instance hackers tricking users into giving their passwords by pretending to call from an IT help desk. Hackers also telephone bona fide help desks in the hope of getting useful information. Caller verification often involves no more than asking for a name and staff identification number, which can be obtained merely by reading an employee's ID card in a local snack bar.

5.8.2 How hackers loot or disrupt a system

1. Viruses and worms. Viruses are self-replicating computer programs or codes used to infect and manipulate a computer or network. Easily written, disguised as normal programmes, spread by e-mail attachments or infected discs, a virus can delete or corrupt all data on a computer system. In some instances a virus lies dormant until a specific date. Worms are technically distinct but similar in effect. The bad publicity caused by virus attacks can be far more damaging to a business than any direct financial loss. Viruses often disguise themselves with a 'rootkit' (a program designed to take fundamental control of a computer system without authorisation by the system's owners) which disables the security programs and searches the hard drive for addresses to send itself to. This makes the computer a 'zombie' infecting other computers on the internet or network. A recent example is the 'Storm' virus (a virus used by hackers to capture the users' activity on line, including log in credentials to banking sites, and forward this information to them in a discreet manner).

2. Keystroke recording programs are implanted by viruses or special hardware (eg a key logger) whereupon they capture everything typed into a PC and e-mail it to the hacker. This nullifies encryption programs since data is captured before encryption takes place.

3. Denial-of-service attacks. A firewall is pelted with thousands of messages in short order so that:

    (a) the firewall is unable to cope and shuts down, severing the company's IT links to the outside world; or
    (b) communications continue but become highly vulnerable to virus infection, or
    (c) the firewall stays up but communications are slowed down.

5.8.3 Making it easy for hackers

Hackers do not always have high levels of technical skill. Bad security practices make IT fraud and abuse alarmingly easy. Here are some examples.

1. IT departments often install software without changing default passwords. So an operating system is installed with the same name for both the user account and password. A hacker will easily gain access if the account is not removed or the password changed.

2. Customers often fail to apply manufacturer supplied 'patches' to close security holes or remove programming bugs.

3. Many organisations fail to monitor the bulletin boards set up by security organisations to warn of new threats and weakness.

4. Many IT departments install software to detect and report hacking attempts but then fail to check the reports or notify senior management of any problems.

5. Outsourcing IT functions can also create opportunities for external fraud if management permits gaps in the control process.

5.9 Other external internet frauds and abuses

1. Bogus websites. 'Phishing' is perhaps the best-known form of internet fraud. Bulk e-mailings purporting to represent a well-known business (such as a bank). The aim is to attract victims to a 'look-alike' website where they can be tricked into disclosing their bank details. Businesses also suffer when they fail to register a specific internet provider address alongside their domain name. Fraudsters can then direct web searchers to a fake site with the same address, or forge letters to the registration authority in order to reallocate a domain name to an IP address under their control. More recently a new form of this type of internet fraud has arisen. Called 'spear fishing' it is tailored to chase people who have been victims to prior phishing scams.

2. Premium rate scam. A number of users are still connected to the internet via modem access. This scam works by discretely disconnecting the user from the Internet Service Provider and making the modem call a premium-rate number for internet access. It is often undertaken while the innocent party is downloading from a website.

3. Hoaxes and chain letters have caused some companies as much trouble as real viruses. Each hoax needs to be investigated and employees tend to clutter up e-mail systems by warning each other of the latest 'threat'.

THE 'EXPLODING' E-MAIL

A help desk was swamped with calls from staff who had received an e-mail claiming that an electrical charge from a new virus could cause PCs to blow up. It claimed that several users had already been injured by broken glass.

5.10   Internet abuse by employees

1. Downloads and e-mails. Staff make extensive personal use of both internet and e-mail, usually with their employer's blessing. But a lack of clear policies on appropriate use often causes problems. Pornography is widespread on the internet and even sophisticated filtering systems cannot always prevent employees downloading it. Both employee and employer run the risk of criminal prosecution if certain materials are then circulated throughout the organisation. Offensive material has also led to civil actions for harassment and discrimination.

2. Theft of IT resources costs organisations large sums of money. There is a difference between the employee who uses his computer for occasional personal use and one who makes a living out of it. One employee distributed illegal video content using the office network. He simply plugged his own server into the office network and made use of the high-speed connection to run his 'business'.

3. Software theft and unauthorised copying is against the law in most jurisdictions. The UK Copyright, Designs and Patents Act 1988 does not distinguish between duplication for sale and free distribution. The manufacture, possession, importation and distribution of illegal software can result in significant fines or even imprisonment, and civil damages can also be extensive. National software industry associations actively seek to bring cases in order to recover lost revenues.

BACKDATED BILLS

A large corporation faced backdated claims of over £13 million for not keeping proper records on the number of software licences it had in use. These were subsequently negotiated down to a six-figure bill. A trawl in another part of the company revealed potential for substantial additional claims.

PIRATES

A company found that one of its employees had copied and sold software to other companies. The relevant trade body agreed not to prosecute on condition that the company undertook a thorough search for unlicensed software. It also had to introduce controls to prevent future breaches of copyright.

5.10.1   Defending the system

Basic measures such as segregation of duties, password protection and control of physical access used to be enough to protect a system. Security was essentially just a matter for the IT people. Powerful, networked and internet-linked PCs on almost every desk have made this regime not only outdated but dangerous. Information Technology is the most effective business enabler available today, but failure to recognise and mitigate the associated risks has disastrous consequences. The following pages explore how proper IT security and fraud detection technologies and controls can help address them.

5.10.2   The centrality of management

The process of identifying, understanding and addressing IT risks demands the combined efforts of business management, IT service and security departments, and the active cooperation of all employees. Only senior managers can ensure that this happens. Information security awareness is a must and therefore should be considered an integral part of the businesses senior manager's responsibilities.

This in turn requires good relationships and lines of communication with both IT and IT security departments (which may operate in a different part of the business). Apparently minor matters such as keeping name and contact details up to date and to hand are in fact vital. When problems do arise there may be little time to act.

5.11   Levels of IT control

Figure 5.2 shows the three levels of IT control.

5.11.1   Application controls

Inherent controls can be implemented at the application level. These reflect the different operations in the business, eg implementation of a maker-checker (segregation between the person inputting a transaction and the person authorising the transaction) electronic work flow for the approval of key transactions.

5.11.2   Information security controls

These control system and application access rights. Standards and guidelines are available to support the security manager in hardening the electronic perimeter against unauthorised and fraudulent access to

Figure 5.2 Layers of IT and related anti-fraud controls

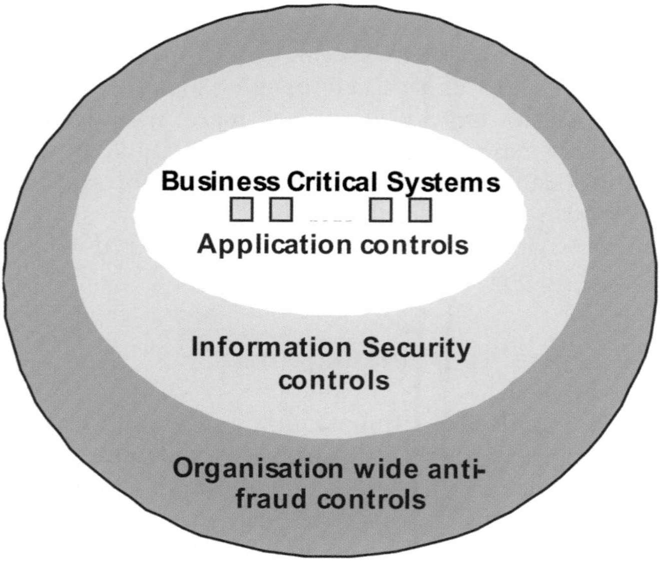

business-critical systems. These include ISO 27001/2 standards (specifications for an Information Security Management System and a code of practice for information security) and National Institute of Standards and Technology guidelines.

5.11.3 Organisation-wide anti-fraud controls

Once application and information security controls are in place the business should have the ability to analyse any interactions with its core systems. This will determine whether they are part of normal business activities or suspicious activities/behaviour. Automated fraud detection technologies can play a vital part in protecting the business.

5.11.4 IT risk management

IT security depends on good risk management. Regular review points are required for every aspect of the system. Each area either generates changes, and therefore a need to reconsider security, or throws up problems indicating weakness in existing controls.

Risk assessment facilitates identification of threats and vulnerabilities, together with estimates of the likelihood and value of losses or other impacts from security breaches. Once these are understood appropriate policies and controls can be selected, designed and implemented. It is management's job to ensure these measures are monitored, measured and audited. The information gained must then be fed back into a review process which reconsiders risks and alters policies and controls as appropriate.

Selection of policies and controls will depend on many factors, including the level of risk that an organisation is willing to accept, business culture, operating environment, industry type, and legal and regulatory requirements. There are many good sources of guidance for security controls, notably British Standard 7799 'Code of Practice for Information Security Management'.

Figure 5.3 IT security management life cycle

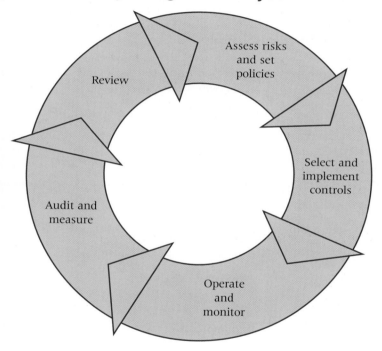

5.11.5 Staff – a crucial line of defence

Good people management is essential to building the levels of assurance necessary in a technology-dependent business. A comprehensive staff IT security and fraud awareness programme is essential. Components of the programme could be included during staff induction sessions and be followed by annual online self-assessment tests.

5.11.6 Incident assessment and response

Organisations will need to ensure any incidents, particularly those involving abuse or deception are assessed and dealt with as soon as possible.

This requires ensuring there is a clear incident assessment and response plan which takes into account not only the financial implications but also reputation and regulatory factors, where appropriate.

In addition, logging and escalation procedures must be clear to ensure appropriate management input and oversight.

5.11.7 Ensuring IT discipline

As will now be apparent, too many organisations neglect basic aspects of IT security. These security aspects include the following.

1. Segregation of computer-related duties and responsibilities.

2. Keeping passwords confidential and changing them periodically.

3. Restricting non-IT staff's physical access to computer facilities.

4. Prohibiting the introduction of external disks and programs without appropriate safeguards.

5. Strict policies and procedures for the reporting of viruses.

6. Clear and rigorous controls over program changes.

7. Clear assessment and response guidelines.

The most expensive and up-to-date systems will not be enough to protect the business unless managers understand the importance of basic disciplines.

5.12 Using IT to fight fraud

It is common to set value parameters for transactions in order to reduce errors or impose authorisation limits, but there are other opportunities for IT to be actively used in fighting fraud and abuse.

Data mining and analysis involves search and comparison programs that are used to find unusual data patterns or inconsistencies across systems. The programs can also perform 'sanity checks' on file permissions and report suspect ones, check password breakability, discover dormant user IDs and highlight potentially weak configuration settings.

5.12.1 Case study – identifying internal fraud via data analytics

Background

An insurance company audit uncovered a number of fraudulent payments being diverted by an employee to their personal bank account. In order to assess the extent of the fraud the company used data analytics to scan all payment transactions for irregularities.

Techniques

Figure 5.4 provides an overview of the steps taken by the insurance company in analysing its payment transactions.

Figure 5.4 Analysis of payment transactions

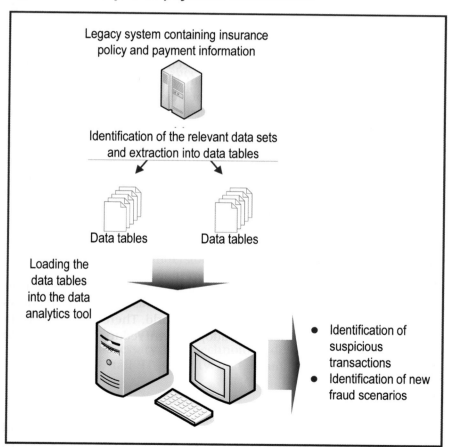

Legacy system containing insurance policy and payment information

Identification of the relevant data sets and extraction into data tables

Data tables

Data tables

Loading the data tables into the data analytics tool

- Identification of suspicious transactions
- Identification of new fraud scenarios

Once the relevant data sets were identified and the legacy policy management and payment system were considered, proprietary software was

traditional IT security measures, these new technologies can be added to the plethora of techniques available to the business to fight fraud.

6   Accounts manipulation

Accounts manipulation is the misrepresentation, suppression or outright forgery of information required for statutory or management reporting. It can cause huge loss of value even without actual theft. Concealed risks may crystallise with devastating consequences: investors commit funds and managers make major decisions on a false premise; companies lose their reputations and their managements lose credibility; and banks lend money they otherwise would not have lent.

Accounts manipulation continues to be an insidious problem and is aggravated by the absence of independent challenge. Decentralisation of business units can heighten the risk. Financial expertise can be spread too thin with teams merely processing data instead of assessing its validity. This is a particularly important issue for group executives and those running large divisions.

Yet it is a risk scarcely recognised by many boards and one absent from many risk-management models. This may be because accounts manipulation is usually an inside job and recognition of the danger can prompt uncomfortable questions. Too many companies overlook what should be an obvious point: that managers are always likely to regard their own units as being free from the risk of accounts manipulation. Managing the risk must always be the responsibility of the next tier up, and ultimately for the Board and Audit Committee, which must also guard against fraud by senior executives.

6.1   Drivers and warning signs

The fraud triangle (**chapter 3**) sets out the three causative factors of fraud: motivation, opportunity and rationalisation. Greed obviously plays a major part in accounts manipulation, but it can also be undertaken to disguise poor performance or error (and in some cases not with theft in mind). Other motivations can be pressure to meet targets and a desire to stop management or others 'interfering in our business'. Many people rationalise their corrupt behaviour by regarding it as 'normal practice' and somehow legitimate.

Warning signs are as follows.

1.   A blame culture.

2.   A non-transparent culture.

3. Highly leveraged reward structures.

4. Management with a personal interest in the company's share price.

5. No effective independent review of key financial data.

6. Failure to perform basic tasks such as reconciliations, review and sign off (a green light to fraudsters).

7. Parts of profit and loss account based on judgement rather than data.

8. History of preparing over-optimistic forecasts.

9. History of untidy balance-sheet management.

10. Cash-flow problems, possibly involving breach of debt covenants.

11. Revenue or profit growth out of line with the industry, or inconsistent with risk levels. eg high profits from inherently low-risk products.

Figure 6.1 summarises the main risks.

Figure 6.1 Common forms of accounts manipulation

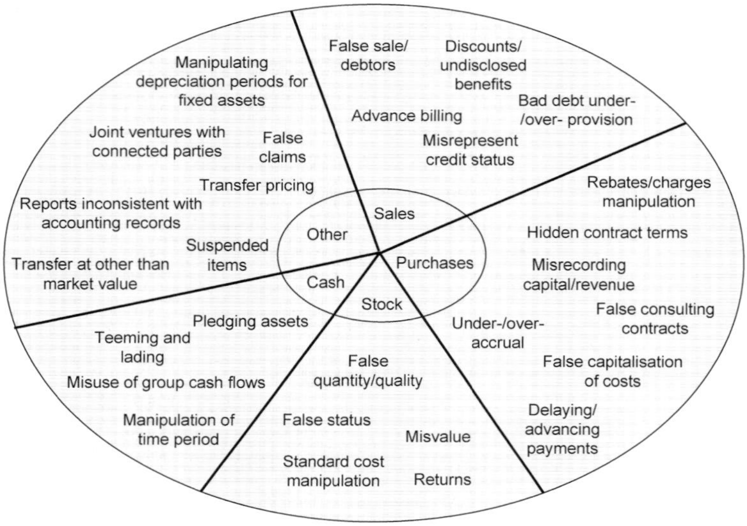

6.2 Sales

6.2.1 False sales

False sales involve manipulation of prices or quantities in order to increase turnover or forecast turnover. A common example is issuing dummy invoices for old or on-display stock in order to allow recognition of a bogus 'profit'. There are many other varieties including the following:

1. Redating old invoices to make them look current.

2. Issuing dummy invoices to fictitious customers.

3. Making sales to 'friendly customers' with an undisclosed agreement to buy back the goods at a later date.

4. Overcharging customers.

5. Kickbacks to customer employees in return for higher prices and/or bigger orders.

6. Phoney sales forecasts and contracts.

7. Forged or suppressed documentation and/or audit confirmations.

Tough business conditions (eg where covenants depend on sales ratios) make false sales frauds more likely.

PAINTING A FALSE PICTURE

The finance director (FD) of a company gave a false picture of his company's financial health to lenders and investors. In fact the accounts had been manipulated by several million pounds by bringing forward revenue for contracted services which had not been provided, together with manipulating asset values and leasing costs. The FD had exercised options during this time. A subsequent investigation uncovered the extent and value of the manipulation resulting in a significant reduction in the company's value.

Look out for the following.

1. Unusual fluctuations in sales, eg high sales in the final quarter.

2. Changes in activity levels inconsistent with underlying data, eg high sales without a change in distribution costs.

3. Changes in business patterns, eg entry into a new and remote market.

4. Shipments to new or unusual customers towards the period end.

5. Cash recycling – payments or deposits coincident with receipt of funds from debtors.

6. Unusual numbers of credit notes around period ends.

7. A large number of journals and adjustments in sales ledgers and/or bank reconciliations.

8. Manual journals and accruals without automatic reversals.

9. Customer not generally known in accounts department; customer details not kept with main filing; account handled directly by senior manager rather than accounts staff.

10. Evasive answers about movements on particular accounts.

6.2.2 Advance billing

This is the bringing forward of sales to boost apparent sales revenue and profits. Common techniques are as follows.

1. Sales recorded in breach of accounting polices.

2. Collusive pre-invoicing, eg advancing sales by routing transactions through connected intermediary companies.

3. Undisclosed sale and return transactions.

4. Stocks 'allocated' to a warehouse under the company's control, or that of a compliant third party, to give the appearance of a sale.

Sometimes advance billing involves misrepresentation about progress or completion of longer-term contracts with a view to inflating turnover or profit. In one case a completion certificate was obtained in return for an undisclosed side letter confirming that outstanding obligations would be performed.

COMPLIANT CUSTOMER

A major Far East electronics manufacturer suffered a sales shortfall in a particular product line. The product manager agreed with the British distributor that a large shipment would be invoiced during the month before the manufacturer's year end. A credit note would be issued several months later, after the manufacturer's audit. The goods were supposedly shipped to a warehouse in the Far East.

PRE-INVOICING

A group got into financial difficulties through product failures and over-extending itself in difficult markets. It could not cover its costs and managers resorted to pre-invoicing of sales via discounted bills of exchange and other financial instruments.

Genuine debtors disappeared from the accounting system, while false sales and sales relating to goods not yet delivered remained on the books. Management accounts did not disclose the substantial use of bills of exchange or the extent to which funds were generated from dealer financing facilities in advance of product manufacture.

By omitting such transactions from the balance sheet, the use of over-draft facilities was minimised, emerging difficulties were obscured and the full extent of the problem was disguised. This worked only until financial losses occurred. The bills then matured and bounced while the management accounts did not recognise liabilities arising from dishonoured bills.

Look out for the following.

1. Inconsistencies in trading patterns, eg delivery costs not fluctuating with deliveries.

2. Merchandising staff reporting high inventory volumes.

3. Unusual changes in debtor ageing profiles.

4. Stocks 'allocated' to customers which go undelivered.

5. Products shipped to destinations other than usual customer addresses.

6. Changes in trading patterns with particularly significant customers.

7. Unusual numbers or values of credit notes subsequent to year end.

6.2.3 Manipulating discounts and other benefits

This allows more subtle forms of fraud. Techniques include the following.

1. Delayed discounts or credits transferred to dummy accounts for write-off.

2. Credits given to customers in the form of reduced current period prices rather than credit notes – with correspondingly higher prices in the following period. This sort of manipulation attracts less attention because it involves fewer people.

3. Taking back non-selling stock at full valuation to avoid a write-off in the current period, followed by hidden promotions in the next.

Look out for:

1. Changes in business patterns with particular customers.

2. Change in prices applied to particular customers around the year end.

3. Unusual numbers or value of credit notes after the year end.

4. Agreements for special advertising (or similar promotional deals) in the following period without any increase in volumes actually shipped.

5. Extended periods of credit for particular customers.

6. Customers dealt with outside the main system, eg no price information on standing data or files held outside main system.

7. Certain customers dealt with exclusively by a senior member of staff.

8. No independent review of prices and terms (or changes thereto) for particular customers.

6.2.4 Manipulation of credit status

This entails:

- suppression of credit information shortly before a sale or deal is concluded;
- supplying false credit status data in order to allow sales to high-risk customers; or
- bribery of credit control staff by sales managers.

Look out for:

- abnormal delays in obtaining routine information;
- sales/commercial staff restricting access to proposed customers;
- poor-quality documentation, eg handwritten paperwork;
- sales staff not sharing information with credit staff; and
- recurrent problems with new credits shortly after sales are concluded.

6.2.5 Bad debt under- or over-provision

This involves:

- misrepresenting the status of particular customers;
- recycling funds to give the impression that a dormant customer account is still active; or
- manipulation of debtor ageing analysis.

> **PROFIT SMOOTHING**
>
> A group had already achieved the level of profit it wished to report but expected the next year to be a lean one. Management therefore invented substantial provisions for a group subsidiary, knowing that the auditors focused on under- rather than over-provision.

Look out for the following.

1. Large cash receipts arriving unexpectedly just before provisions are finalised.

2. No independent check of tagged debtors analysis, sales ledger or bank reconciliations.

3. Inconsistencies between bad-debt write-offs/recovery proceedings.

4. Inconsistencies between debtor ageing profile and proposed provisioning/unusual trends in report profile during the year.

6.3 Purchases

There are many different forms of purchasing frauds. A number of these involve a direct manipulation of the accounts and these are set out below. Further details on purchasing fraud are set out in chapter 7.

6.3.1 Manipulation of rebates and discounts

This is a common problem which has increased alongside highly-leveraged supply contracts. Examples include the following.

1. Taking a rebate to profit too early because it is conditional on guaranteed levels of business with the supplier. Contract terms can be hidden or confined to side letters.

2. Extra charges paid in the current period returned as a rebate in the following period.

3. Postponed charges.

4. Misrepresentation/forging of rebate confirmations and contract details.

Look out for:

- lack of openness about negotiation process and deal details;

- restricted access to supplier;

- budgets developed and applied late in the accounting period;

- surplus stock levels allowed to trigger volume discounts;

- significant increases/reductions in supplier charges in the following period;

- highly-leveraged supply contracts negotiated by a handful of staff;

- no independent review of the need for goods/services supplied; and

- deliveries taken at unusual times of the year.

6.3.2 Hidden contract terms and side letters

These are used in many business areas.

Look out for:

- unexpected completions ahead of schedule;
- unusual trends in results prior to year end;
- resistance to direct contact with supplier about account balances or terms;
- late changes in allocations between capital and revenue;
- suppliers billing unusual items, eg revenue items appearing as capital ones; and
- unusual leasing arrangements or lessors who cannot be verified.

6.3.3 Misrecording of capital or revenue items

This is one of the better-known forms of manipulation. It is vital to probe further if a case is discovered because this is likely to be part of a wider problem.

INFLATED WORTH

A company stretched itself to the limit in funding an acquisition. The chairman and finance director responded by inflating their company's worth by over £250 million. This involved the following.

1. Treating a rebate on the acquisition purchase price as income (which in turn caused inflated profit expectations).

2. Booking credit notes as sales.

3. Capitalising unwarranted research and development.

4. Inflating valuations of corporate assets.

5. Falsely claiming to have sold an overseas subsidiary.

A projected £10.5 million profit was later reported to be a £23 million loss and the share price collapsed from £2.26 to 10p.

Look out for the following.

1. Unusual trends in individual work-in-progress accounts.

2. Evidence of operational difficulties or unknown counterparties.

3. Excessive pressure to deliver results, especially when combined with factors such as an impending unit closure.

4. Nervous or vague responses to detailed questions.

5. An unclear audit trail between management accounts and the general ledger.

6. Long-standing systems problems.

6.3.4 Accruals or provisions manipulation

This is one of the easiest frauds to commit, though given the visibility of accruals it ought also to be one of the easiest to spot. It can also provide the first clue to wider problems.

The companies most vulnerable to this type of fraud are those with poor linkage between budgets and underlying activities, eg the budget for a particular area is based on a percentage of turnover rather than on a bottom-up assessment of required spend. Problems can be compounded unless transfers between individual budget areas are closely controlled.

Other common problems include the following.

1. Accruing actual to budget in monthly management accounts. This is usually linked to forward purchase orders and collusive pre-invoicing with suppliers at year end.

2. Concealed supplier invoices.

3. Over- or understating the cost of goods received.

4. Poor reconciliation of accruals for goods received but not yet invoiced.

Look out for the following.

1. Changes in creditor age profile.

2. Changes in purchasing patterns just before and after year end.

3. 'Soft' budgets based on a percentage of turnover without zero-basing.

4. Transfers between budgets and actual figures to manipulate under- and over-spends.

5. Little or no budget/actual variances.

6. Unusual trends on particular budget captions, eg a significant under-spend up to Q3 and budget fully utilised by the end of the period.

6.3.5 Consulting and other service contracts

These provide an ideal opportunity for creating false costs because there may be little tangible evidence of the service provided. False consulting contracts for acquisition assistance, bid defence work, public relations, design, introductions to new markets, etc. can also be used to manipulate reported results. Costs may be accrued or paid to a connected or bogus counterparty for future use in the business. They can also be a way of cloaking unauthorised, illegal or corrupt activity.

Look out for the following.

1. Significant increase in consulting payments without evidence of increased activity or value.

2. Invoices with vague descriptions of services provided.

3. Invoices from previously unknown suppliers, particularly if their status cannot be readily verified.

There is more on dummy supplier frauds in **chapter 7**.

6.3.6 False capitalisation of costs

This can involve elaborate deception and collusion by a number of parties. Examples include:

- forged or manipulated documents to support capitalisation criteria;

- costs misdescribed on invoices, or

- journals between expense and fixed assets in the ledger accounts.

Look out for the following.

1. Evasive responses or delaying tactics when documents are requested.

2. Senior managers handling administrative details which would usually be delegated.

6.3.7 Non-standard terms

These are a common way of shifting profits between periods. Suppliers may be happy to comply if they have cash-flow problems or want a favour. Problems include the following.

1. Non-standard payment or other terms agreed in order to reduce or inflate apparent prices charged to the profit and loss account in the current or next period.

2. Misrepresentation of creditor ageing.

Look out for the following signs.

1. Contracts bypassing normal negotiation or contract procedures.

2. Oral evidence from accounts staff of particular payments being advanced or delayed.

3. Changes in the company's cash-flow profile.

4. Changes in pricing and margins around period ends.

6.4 Stock

6.4.1 Misvaluation

Over-valuation of stock is a recognised form of accounts manipulation; under-valuation is less well known. Where management has already hit current year targets and/or bonus thresholds, it may try to tuck away some profits for use in a less favourable period. Such practices can be orchestrated at group level by setting 'required' profits levels and then manipulating stock and other figures to meet them.

Such practices are widespread yet disbelief that this can occur often results in management failing to acknowledge their existence. This is doubly dangerous as they provide the perfect cover for other frauds. Typical activities are as follows.

1. Over- or under-valuation of raw materials.

2. Over- or under-valuation of work-in-progress.

3. Losses on unprofitable contracts credited against the work-in-progress of profitable ones.

The following examples demonstrate how manipulation can become embedded in corporate culture.

BLACK HOLE

A new financial controller came under intense pressure from top management to achieve budgeted results in spite of the loss of a large contract which had accounted for a quarter of budgeted turnover.

An operations director indicated that stock values were on the low side. The financial controller began to overstate them without seeking substantive justification and so brought profit back within budget.

Half-way through the year the financial controller was tasked with closing down a site. At year-end he was refused a bonus and he retaliated by adding spurious names to the redundancy list, payments for which went into his own pocket. By the year end he had overstated profits by approximately £5 million and stolen about £25,000.

Look out for the following.

1. Profit or bonus targets reached in the latter part of the year followed by a flat performance thereafter.

2. New explanations for stock saleability and market conditions.

3. Unusual trends in the valuation of particular stock lines, work in progress and/or margins.

6.4.2 False status

This can often be linked to misvaluation frauds. These include:

- forging or filtering information about realisable stock values and potential disposals;
- misrepresenting stock ownership;
- colluding with a third party to borrow stock around period ends; and
- stock sold or leased during an inventory while being counted as unsold.

Look out for the following things.

1. New or unexpected explanations for realisable values.

2. Obsolete or slow-moving stock lines suddenly finding new outlets, eg an emerging market where the status of the counterparty and distribution channel are clouded in secrecy.

6.4.3 Falsification of stock quantities

Manipulation in this area takes the following forms:

- forged stocktake sheets; and
- counting already sold stock in inventories.

The following represents a typical case.

FICTITIOUS STOCK

A lean head office devolved operating responsibility to subsidiaries and put them under considerable pressure to perform.

In order to hit targets one finance director increased notional stock volumes for lines held at the year end which had gone uncounted by the auditors.

When the fraud came to light the resultant 'black hole' cast doubt over the whole group's results. Its share price fell significantly and some top managers lost their jobs.

Look out for the following.

1. Management monitoring which stock lines are being checked by auditors.

2. Different handwriting on stock sheets purporting to be a sequence counted by a single person.

3. Unusual trends in stock levels.

6.4.4   Manipulation of quality data

This involves false documentation and suppression of information. It frequently involves bribery of, and collusion with, internal or external quality inspectors. Stock requiring expert valuation or liable to deterioration is particularly at risk.

Manipulation may be linked to collusive substandard, or bogus product, frauds on the purchasing or sales sides.

Look out for:

- changes in inspection staff;

- poor-quality supporting documentation; and

- purely oral reports or delayed supporting documentation.

6.4.5   Standard cost manipulation

Standard costing systems are prone to manipulation.

Look out for:

- late adjustments to standard costs; and

- changes in standard costs inconsistent with sales/general costs.

6.5   Cash

The frauds discussed here focus on moving funds around a group to inflate asset values and overstate sales.

6.5.1   Asset pledging

This is usually undertaken in return for temporary cash flow. For instance, a bank places a deposit with another in the same group. The second bank then lends money to a nominated beneficiary with the deposit as security. No record is made of the first bank's deposit or the contingent liability arising from the loan. This conceals the exposure while appearing to satisfy liquidity regulations by notionally adding to funds on deposit. Loan proceeds can of course be channelled back to the bank, eg to make it appear that bad loans are performing.

Look out for:

- deposits inconsistent with business activity;

- rollover of deposits held by individual banks;

- unusual counterparties;

- changes in debtor receipt patterns, eg debtors pledged and refinanced; and

- deposits that are an unusual size.

6.5.2 'Teeming and lading'

This is a well-known sales fraud involving the theft of cash or cheque receipts on a sales ledger. The fraudster conceals unpaid amounts until he is able to repay them or until he disappears. These are sometimes referred to as 'lapping' frauds. Similar manipulations can take place in purchasing and are also used in the cash area to manipulate a company's financial position. Further details on this type of fraud appear in section 7.2.5.

TAKING A CUT

The finance manager in a media business stole funds received from a long-standing client. He used the subsequent payment from the same client to match against the first debt when preparing journal entries. He continued this process throughout the year thus always being at least one payment behind. The manager repeated this process on a number of client accounts netting him a sizeable amount of cash which he diverted for personal use.

The frauds were uncovered some time later when one of the customers queried amounts due.

Look out for the following.

- account or fee note numbers which do not match;

- reconciliations where unreconciled amounts are not appropriately followed up; and

- timing differences between date of invoice and date settled.

6.5.3 Misuse of group cash flows

A group can disguise the need for bad-debt provisions in one operation by transferring cash from another. This is sometimes combined with other forms of manipulation such as suspending items in unreconciled inter-company accounts.

Associates or joint venture companies are particularly attractive targets when their results are not consolidated in group figures. The following is an elaborate example.

FICTITIOUS CONTRACT

Two directors, one of whom was a finance director, realised that a delay to a long-term contract would stop them hitting their earn-out targets.

They responded by setting up a fake contract in an emerging market, creating customer receipts together with suppliers and subcontractors to whom payments could be made. Funds were transferred against false invoices generated by the finance director. These were transferred to a real bank account for a fictitious customer, then returned to the company for which the two directors worked.

As advance customer payments were normally expected for one type of contract the directors used a 25 per cent joint venture company which was effectively under their control with its own auditors and year end. Its general manager received funds and returned them with payment instructions indicating they had been received from the fictitious customer.

Look out for the following.

1. Large movements in cash through inter-company, associate or joint venture accounts.

2. Asset transfers through inter-company, associate or joint venture accounts.

3. Customers and suppliers with the same or similar names or principals.

4. Large values for cash-in-transit.

5. Bank reconciliations where the account balance at period end does not equate with the ledger balance, or where the account is not used in the reconciliation.

6. Unusual patterns in foreign exchange transactions.

6.6 Other forms of manipulation

6.6.1 Transfers at other than market value

These have featured in many international accounts manipulation cases. Typical cases include:

- assets exchanged for shares at inflated values;

- values increased or decreased by moving assets around a group; and

- assets acquired with concealed or understated liabilities.

Look out for:

- frequent movements of assets amongst group companies;
- asset movements lacking commercial or tax reasons; and
- asset transactions with offshore/tax-haven companies.

6.6.2 Suspending items

Suspending items in inter-company accounts is one of the more obvious forms of manipulation. It is often overlooked because reconciling inter-company accounts is seen as a tiresome job.

Even where reconciliations appear to have been carried out they may simply camouflage irregular activity through inter-company accounts. It is therefore important to review the underlying nature of the transactions.

Look out for the following.

1. Significant reconciling items in inter-company, branch or joint-venture accounts.
2. Photocopied or faxed confirmations received from other parts of the group.
3. Poorly documented reconciliations offering unclear reasoning.
4. Accounts staff unaware of the reasons for certain items going through inter-company accounts.

6.6.3 Joint ventures and other alliances

These may be used to inflate or depress the results of either party for a particular period. Sometimes a joint venture is set up specifically for this purpose (as shown in the 'Fictitious contract' example above).

Look out for the following.

1. New joint ventures late in a period.
2. Unclear reasons for a joint venture.
3. Most staff knowing little or nothing about a joint venture.
4. Joint venture not governed in an appropriate manner.
5. Joint ventures with residential addresses; addresses identical to that of a another supplier, employee, employee's close relative or former employer.

Figure 7.1 Typical purchasing frauds

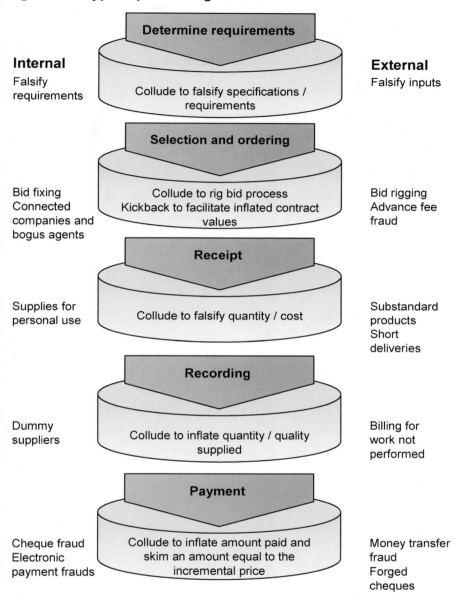

Internal

Falsify requirements

Bid fixing
Connected companies and bogus agents

Supplies for personal use

Dummy suppliers

Cheque fraud
Electronic payment frauds

Determine requirements

Collude to falsify specifications / requirements

Selection and ordering

Collude to rig bid process
Kickback to facilitate inflated contract values

Receipt

Collude to falsify quantity / cost

Recording

Collude to inflate quantity / quality supplied

Payment

Collude to inflate amount paid and skim an amount equal to the incremental price

External

Falsify inputs

Bid rigging
Advance fee fraud

Substandard products
Short deliveries

Billing for work not performed

Money transfer fraud
Forged cheques

discounts. External frauds include billing for unperformed work and over-billing.

5. Payment. Payments must be made only in respect of authorised invoices. Proper security must also be maintained over cheque-books and the use of money transfer systems.

7.1.2 Internal purchasing frauds

Internal purchasing fraud occurs because of false requirements for goods and services. Potential suppliers can also collude with staff to develop specifications which only the former can fulfil.

> **CONTRACTOR'S DELIGHT**
>
> The manager of a business unit colluded with a management services consultancy to provide advice on market segmentation. The company had no real need for the services (and indeed no service was provided) but decisions made at the specification stage ensured the contractor was awarded the project.

Look out for:

- poorly defined or undefined specifications; and

- relevant staff not aware of goods and services being supplied, or of the need for them.

Bid fixing

In this type of fraud bidders obtain inside information, usually in return for a kickback. The information may be about selection criteria, technical specifications or other bids. The purchaser pays more and obtains less-favourable terms than if a truly competitive process had taken place. In some cases the specifications for an entire project may have been compromised as inappropriate equipment will have been purchased.

In larger contracts so-called 'information brokers' can act as intermediaries between employees leaking confidential information and tendering companies who wish to buy it. The brokers serve to conceal the source of the leak. Kickbacks may also be concealed via offshore front companies and/or numbered accounts in countries with strict banking secrecy laws.

> **INFORMATION BROKERS AT WORK**
>
> Employees in a major civil engineering company passed selection criteria and the prices of other bids to 'information brokers' who in turn sold the information to a potential supplier. This enabled the potential supplier to pitch a price 10 per cent (£20 million) higher than it would otherwise have submitted.

Look out for the following.

1. Abnormal prices or terms, eg specifications which can only be met by one supplier.

2. Separate bid prices clustered closely together.

3. Well-known suppliers not being invited to tender.

4. Pre-qualified suppliers.

5. Different bidders having common personnel, addresses or solicitors.

6. Waivers of normal business terms and conditions.

7. A small supplier handling a large contract.

8. A remote supplier used for routine services.

9. A supplier providing services beyond its normal range of business.

10. Tenders accepted after the closing date.

11. High levels of extras/claims by particular suppliers.

12. Changes to specifications or prices soon after a contract is awarded.

13. Suppliers issuing a large number of invoices just beneath the purchaser's approval threshold, thereby avoiding more formal tendering procedures.

14. Procurement staff who become unduly defensive when asked about contracts.

15. Failure to debrief former suppliers and unsuccessful bidders.

Kickbacks and inducements

Kickbacks and inducements are used in many types of purchasing fraud to favour particular suppliers. They can be difficult to detect because the evidence, if any, may only be found in the supplier's own records. This is why contracts sometimes provide for the vendor's right to audit key supplier accounts such as entertaining. The warning signs of this kind of fraud are the same as those for bid fixing.

BROWN ENVELOPES

A supplier's managing director bribed directors and executives of a cooperative for 12 years in order to hold on to business worth £300,000 a week. The bribes took the form of cash, exotic holidays and prostitutes. The supplier made up for these expenses by charging the cooperative above market rate. The fraud was eventually discovered when the customer started rejecting the supplier's produce on quality grounds.

Connected companies

Prices or quantities may be manipulated or products substituted by intermediaries. This is most likely to happen where the intermediary is acting for an overseas supplier with whom it is difficult to have direct contact. Unnecessary or exorbitant charges may be built into the price.

THE MIDDLEMAN'S SHARE

A purchasing manager set up a bogus print-buying company and awarded it his group's business, adding a 100 per cent mark-up to underlying supplier prices. He got away with the fraud due to poor budgeting procedures, weak scrutiny of marketing costs by finance and senior management, plus the absence of any independent review of suppliers, the services they supplied and the basis of their pricing.

Look out for:

- intermediaries of unknown ownership or status;

- unclear reasons for intermediary arrangements; and

- no independent monitoring of vendor complaints.

Work done/goods supplied for private purposes

This is one of the most common purchasing frauds. The risk is increased when activities are poorly supervised and when materials are readily transferable to other uses.

HOME IMPROVEMENTS

Staff in a maintenance department incorporated work on their own homes into official schedules. They removed supplies from inventory and falsified time records, even charging overtime for the work carried out on their own properties.

Look out for:

- unusual delivery times or methods;

- ambiguous or abbreviated descriptions on invoices;

- over-ordered or surplus stock lines;

- weak links between invoices and the origination of an order; and

- poor segregation of duties.

Dummy suppliers

Companies often have strong controls over initial supplier selection but fail to look out for inflated or phoney invoices. Computer installations, office refurbishments, maintenance, design and other consultancy work can be particular problem areas for this type of fraud.

There are many variations on the dummy supplier theme. Payments are made for services that are never provided. Monies are posted to accounts which the supplier no longer uses. Dummy sub-accounts or branches may be set up to make it harder to identify unusual suppliers or supplies. Amounts may be posted to 'off budget' accounts (such as recharge accounts) or 'up-front' payments/deposits made in respect of bogus contracts. 'Teeming and lading' involves the fraudster changing the payee detail on an incoming cheque or setting up a bank account in a supplier's name, diverting the cheque and using subsequent cheques made payable to the supplier to 'settle' the earlier unpaid liability.

Look out for the following.

1. Unclear reasons for particular supplies and few details about services provided.

2. Suppliers not generally known to staff, not handled in normal way, or dealt with exclusively by a single person.

3. Suppliers with the same address as another supplier.

4. Invoices which are soiled, incomplete, over-abbreviated or altered.

5. Unfolded invoices: this can indicate that they have not been sent in the post.

6. Corporate suppliers with no VAT number or an incorrect one.

7. Suppliers issuing a large number of invoices just beneath the purchaser's approval threshold.

8. Numerous contras or other adjustments on the purchase ledger.

9. Numerous entries in suspense accounts during the year.

10. Resistance to requests to confirm supplier accounts.

11. Suppliers not offering usual discounts or special deals.

12. Weak account-opening procedures or weak controls over amendments to standing data.

13. Poor control over dormant supplier accounts.

14. Poor controls for paid invoices.

15. No zero-based budgets.

16. No clearly defined budget holders for particular accounts.

Misuse of credit notes, rebates and volume discounts

Purchase costs may be manipulated in two ways. Credit notes may be used to manipulate profits or to conceal other frauds. Volume discounts and rebates can be triggered artificially and diverted for the fraudster's benefit.

Look out for the following.

1. Abnormal numbers and/or value of credit notes around period ends.

2. Volume discounts/rebates not monitored independently against quantities of goods bought.

3. Stock surpluses (indicating possible over-purchasing) used to trigger volume discounts.

7.1.3 External purchasing frauds

Bid rigging

This entails supplier manipulation of the competitive bidding process. Bidders typically conspire to fix prices and terms for particular contracts which are then rotated between them.

Advance fee fraud

Advance fee fraud has attracted a good deal of publicity in recent years. The fraudster takes an up-front fee or deposit for goods or services and then disappears. Businesses most at risk are those having difficulty in obtaining a particular product or service, notably credit. The fraudster tempts them with low rates or prices while usually avoiding doing business face to face.

A particularly prevalent form involves bogus credit facilities. The fraudster promises that, on payment of a fee, he will either fund directly at a low rate of interest or put the borrower in touch with a lender. The advance fee is supposed to pay legal expenses and facilitate the loan and/or to confirm the borrower's intentions. Needless to say both funds and lender are non-existent.

The borrower is asked to sign a non-disclosure, non-circumvention or 'specific performance' agreement. If he fails to comply with the 'lender's' conditions – and these are designed to be impossible to meet – he is deemed to have defaulted and the advance payment is forfeited.

Blocked funds

This involves inducing depositors to place funds with a scheme by showing them a document called a 'blocked funds letter' that is supposed to have been created by a bank. It states that the promoters have a significant amount of collateral with which to raise loans. The letter goes on to say that the funds are available 'with full bank authority' and are 'blocked for a number of banking days and free of all liens or encumbrances over the period'. No returns are forthcoming.

Look for the following signs:

- abnormally low prices for goods/services;

- requirements for non-returnable up-front payments or deposits;

- all dealings conducted through agents;

- impossible to verify authenticity of documentation;

- complex and/or unusual financial instruments;

- the purported principal being overseas and/or an inability to reveal his identity; and

- agent in a hurry to conclude the deal.

Short deliveries/invoicing for goods or services not supplied

Companies at greatest risk are those with:

- weak controls over goods received;

- poor physical security;

- weak account-opening procedures; and

- weak links between origination of order, receipt of goods and approval of invoice.

USING THE MISCELLANEOUS ACCOUNT

A marketing director with a multi-million pound promotions budget took bribes to approve invoices from four suppliers for work which had not been done, or which was for more than amounts actually due. He hid the fraud by debiting the money from the company's 'miscellaneous' account rather than his own budget. The fraud was discovered as a result of concerns raised by a sales promotion manager.

Look out for:

- excessive budgets;

- stock shortages;

- deliveries at unusual times or to unusual locations; and

- signs of tampering with measuring equipment.

Substandard product fraud

This can be devastating where the substandard products involve sophisticated equipment. Companies most at risk are those lacking rigorous quality-control checks on goods supplied or independent checks on the credentials and capabilities of key suppliers. Risks are higher when suppliers are changed at the last moment, during rushed jobs or where terms require substantial advance payment. Dishonest suppliers sometimes make grandiose claims about work supposedly performed for major public companies or governments. It is surprising how often these are accepted at face value.

Billing for work not performed/over-billing

Contracts involving a large number of invoices, where a service is supplied at a remote location or where it is hard to check performance of individual project stages are especially vulnerable to these types of fraud.

PADDING THE INVOICES

A businessman paid hundreds of thousands of pounds in bribes over four years to an employee of a major car manufacturer, in return for lucrative artwork contracts. The employee held an annual budget of £2.5 million. Another manager in the technical publications department worked with him and received £25,000 'hush money', lavish lunches and free flights to France. A middleman negotiated contracts on their behalf and also put work out to genuine subcontractors while submitting vastly inflated invoices. The company received a tip-off and launched an investigation.

Look out for:

- no independent checks on prices or volume discounts;
- no competitive tendering;
- no zero-based budgeting;
- vague contract terms; and
- no detailed review of charges in areas such as travel, advertising, consultancy fees, recruitment, maintenance and leasing.

7.2   Sales fraud

There are four main phases in a typical sales cycle:

- receipt of the sales order;
- delivery of goods or services;
- invoicing and recording of the sale; and
- payment.

The following figure provides examples of internal, external and collusive fraud risks in the sales process.

Figure 7.2 Typical sales frauds

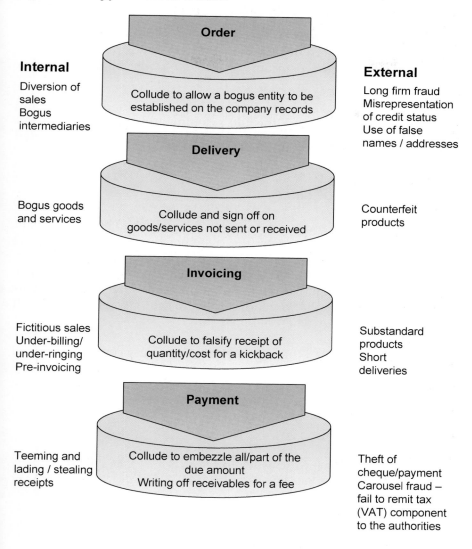

Internal

Diversion of
sales
Bogus
intermediaries

Order

Collude to allow a bogus entity to be
established on the company records

External

Long firm fraud
Misrepresentation
of credit status
Use of false
names / addresses

Delivery

Bogus goods
and services

Collude and sign off on
goods/services not sent or received

Counterfeit
products

Invoicing

Fictitious sales
Under-billing/
under-ringing
Pre-invoicing

Collude to falsify receipt of
quantity/cost for a kickback

Substandard
products
Short
deliveries

Payment

Teeming and
lading / stealing
receipts

Collude to embezzle all/part of the
due amount
Writing off receivables for a fee

Theft of
cheque/payment
Carousel fraud –
fail to remit tax
(VAT) component
to the authorities

1. Order phase. It is vital to ensure that orders are not diverted and to ascertain whether customers are misrepresenting their identity or credit status. Internal frauds include diversion of sales and the use of bogus intermediary companies to manipulate margins and 'cream off' profits. External frauds include the use of false names and addresses by customers and the misrepresentation of credit status.

2. Delivery phase. The main concern here is that the customer receives what he ordered. Major frauds in this phase of the cycle include non-delivery, supply of substandard goods or services, and short deliveries. External frauds include counterfeiting of branded

products. Collusion results in the business taking substandard, short-supplied, over-priced goods or services.

3. Invoicing phase. Goods and services must be properly invoiced and invoices must represent real sales. Internal frauds include fictitious sales, kickbacks to or from customers, under-billing and pre-invoicing.

4. Payment phase. Payments need to be collected, deposited and recorded. Internal frauds include 'teeming and lading' and corrupt writing off of receivables. A number of specifically cash-related frauds are dealt with at **7.4**.

7.2.1 Diversion of sales

This usually involves routing sales to companies owned by the fraudster via misuse of mailing lists, diverting customer responses to advertising and promotions, sabotage of customer contracts, offering deliberately uncompetitive terms or intentionally providing poor service. The risk can be particularly high before and after an acquisition or major reorganisation, eg where the vendors stay with the business, where staff have been demoted or when morale is low.

Sales may also be routed through bogus intermediary companies owned by the fraudster or his associates, eg brokers or distributors, with the fraudster taking a cut in the form of hidden commissions or unusual pricing.

SABOTAGE

An ex-director of a company which had been acquired and divisionalised remained with the group but diverted sales to a rival company of his own. He ensured his employer's tenders were non-competitive and gave poor service on existing contracts. He naturally recommended his rival company as an alternative. Management realised something was wrong when several staff left the division and it under-performed against budget.

BOGUS BROKER

A general manager and his deputy told tour companies that they could only charter aircraft through a particular broker. They wrote a bogus price in their employer's accounts while the broker invoiced customers for a higher amount and diverted the difference to a bank account in Zurich. The fraud was discovered through a tip-off, but only after four years.

Look out for the following.

1. Unexpected loss of customers or a high level of customer complaints (assuming such complaints are monitored independently).

2. Inconsistent business patterns, eg main sales fall while spares sales constant (or vice versa).

3. No independent appraisal of pricing structures or amounts charged by intermediaries.

4. No checks on ownership of supplier companies.

7.2.2 Bogus goods and services

Bogus (or substandard) goods and services often slip through when new ventures use unproven employees. Customers are also vulnerable if they find it difficult to appraise the quality of a product or service. Such frauds occur when suppliers, or some of their staff, want to meet profit targets or divert products for unauthorised purposes.

DEADLY DEFECT

A defence company's quality control manager uncovered a defect that could make missiles fall off the aircraft carrying them. He claimed his employer ordered him to conceal the defect. When he was later dismissed he sued the company and notified the authorities. His employer pleaded guilty to conspiracy to defraud.

Look out for the following.

1. Products which are 'too good to be true'.

2. Services provided at remote locations or due at a date far in the future (particularly if requiring up-front payments or deposits).

3. Complex explanations for advantageous pricing.

7.2.3 Kickbacks to or from customers

These involve a benefit in return for manipulating quantities or prices, or supplying a different grade of product. The risk is increased when there is no independent review of prices and/or terms of business. Bribes may also be paid to employees to write off debts, issue credit notes or extend credit.

LUCRATIVE FRANCHISES

Several senior executives and employees at a subsidiary of a major car manufacturer received kickbacks from dealers in return for awarding lucrative franchises and allocations of sought-after car models at times when demand exceeded supply.

Look out for the following.

1. Customers handled outside the main system, eg exclusively by a senior member of staff using non-standard documentation.

2. No pricing information on standing data files.

3. Unusual prices, discounts or credit terms.

4. Unusual margin trends.

5. Alterations to invoices or other documentation.

7.2.4 Under-billing and under-ringing

Under-billing involves the suppression of invoices, the understating of quantities despatched or the manipulation of prices and discounts. Under-ringing is the under-recording of cash sales.

Look out for the following signs.

1. Alterations to delivery notes or invoices.

2. Transactions or customers handled exclusively by one member of staff using non-standard documentation.

3. No sequential or systematic filing of invoices.

4. No independent checks on prices.

5. Weak controls over changes to standing data or the absence of standing data for particular customers.

6. Poor control over 'miscellaneous' sales.

7. Poor control over till rolls.

8. No reconciliation of stock movements to sales.

7.2.5 Teeming and lading/stealing of receipts

Perhaps the best-known sales fraud is 'teeming and lading'. As set out in section 6.5.2 it involves the theft of cash or cheque receipts on a sales ledger, and the use of later receipts (or receipts from other customers) to 'settle' the outstanding amounts. The fraudster conceals the unpaid amounts for as long as possible until he is either able to repay the money he has stolen or until he disappears.

Poor segregation of duties significantly increases the risk. It is important to separate the recording of sales from the handling of cash or cheques, and keep both of these separate from customer complaints.

A CREATIVE ACCOUNTANT

A temporary credit controller stole cheques payable to his employer and paid them into accounts he had opened in the company's name. The fraud was concealed by bogus journal entries and teeming and lading on sales ledger accounts.

'COMPUTER ERROR'

A sales ledger clerk stole a number of cheques, telling customers that outstanding items on their statements were only 'computer errors'. He was discovered when he had to make a significant transfer from another account.

Look out for the following.

1. Part-paid items on the sales ledger.

2. Large numbers of journals or adjustments on particular accounts or on bank reconciliations.

3. Unusual fluctuations or inconsistencies on the aged debtor analysis.

4. Alterations to invoices/frequent issue of 'duplicates' on particular accounts.

5. Differences between original and duplicate paying-in slips, incomplete details or alterations.

6. Differences between paying-in slips, cash book details and ledger postings, eg number of items, dates and payee details.

7. No independent review of customers who do not pay or who delay payment.

8. No independent despatch of statements.

9. No independent investigation of complaints.

7.2.6   Writing off receivables for a fee

Credit controllers or other staff may be bribed by a customer during the collection phase of the cycle in order to write off outstanding debts or to undermine the chances of legal action by introducing complicating factors. One warning sign is a heavy concentration of provisions or write-offs attributable to one employee or division.

7.2.7 Long firm fraud

The fraudster purports to run a bona fide business and so obtains goods on credit, the first orders are small and are paid for quickly. As the supplier's confidence in his new customer increases so does the size of the orders, and further credit is given. When the fraudster believes he has obtained maximum credit he disposes of the goods and disappears, leaving the suppliers in the lurch.

Long company fraud is one of the oldest white-collar crimes. The Victorians complained of the fraudulent activities of 'phantom capitalists'. It tends to be carried on by highly-organised gangs operating through several linked businesses. The risk increases when it is difficult for a supplier to make face-to-face contact with his customer.

> **HERE TODAY, GONE TOMORROW**
>
> A group of fraudsters set up several retail businesses using off-the-shelf companies and false identities. Distinctive headed paper was prepared, orders were placed and credit granted. Some of the references given to suppliers came from fraudster-owned companies which naturally gave glowing testimony to creditworthiness and financial stability.
>
> The first deliveries were paid for promptly and were followed by increased credit and larger orders. The goods went to the fraudsters' own warehouse and sold at discount prices to bargain stores and market traders. After a few months of operation, the fraudsters disappeared leaving the suppliers' bills unpaid.

Look out for:

- an unreal air about the principals/their premises, eg no customer orientation;

- new customers with rapidly increasing turnover, and

- no independent checks on referees.

7.2.8 Misrepresentation of credit status

This includes a wide range of practices involving impersonation or the submission of false or misleading information.

Look out for the following signs.

1. Poor-quality documentation.

2. New customers using 'accommodation' addresses.

3. Customers operating through 'front' companies or intermediaries.

4. Incomplete customer details or undue difficulties in completing normal credit references and other basic information.

7.3 Stock frauds

Stock frauds relating to values, provisions, receipt and despatch have been discussed above. This section considers stock frauds covering the holding of stock and distribution channels.

7.3.1 Theft of stock

This can involve a large number of employees, sometimes in collusion with organised criminals, and may remain undetected for years. Staff or contractors sometimes claim goods were 'damaged' in transit or have exceeded their expiry date, thus ensuring that they are written off, after which the fraudsters sells them on. Companies handling valuable and easily movable products (such as electrical goods and motor vehicle spare parts) are especially vulnerable.

Look out for the following.

1. Unexplained differences between book and physical stock.

2. Inconsistencies between general turnover and that in particular units.

3. Part-loaded delivery vehicles.

4. Drivers asking for routes to be amended or asking to do the same routes.

5. Deliveries received or made at unusual times of the day.

6. No monitoring of stock losses and no regular stock counts.

7. Weak procedures for goods received or despatched.

8. Poor control over stock movements during stocktakes.

9. Poor control over unaccepted or incorrect loads.

10. Payment of storage facilities which are not aligned with normal requirements.

11. No independent follow-up of customer complaints, eg for sub-standard products, delays in delivery or short deliveries.

7.3.2 Theft of returned stock or valuable scrap

This is quite common and rich pickings can be made by the opportunist fraudster especially given the high price of commodities today. In one case partly damaged stock returned to a building materials company was removed and re-sold by warehouse staff. In another an employee tasked with sending high-quality scrap metal for reprocessing colluded with someone at the processing company to falsify metal weights and types.

7.3.3 Metering and weighbridge frauds

This kind of equipment is prone to tampering and regular checks are essential. Frequent breakdowns or faults occurring at unusual times should be investigated thoroughly.

PHONEY TICKETS

A managing director and seven colleagues conspired to defraud a local authority while working on road surfacing contracts worth £2.5 million. The fraud involved issuing fake weighbridge tickets for deliveries of road-building materials which were subsequently incorporated in the invoice sent to the local authority. The company owned a quarry and its weighbridge operators would generate false tickets and drivers' signatures for non-existent loads.

7.4 Cash and payment fraud

There is huge scope for fraud and malpractice in this field. In addition to those discussed here, certain dealing-related frauds described in **chapter 8** may be relevant to treasury departments in larger companies.

7.4.1 Cheque fraud

This involves forged signatures, stolen cheques or cheque-books, misuse of cancelled cheques, unsupported cash advances and the theft of cash or cash equivalents.

DOUBLE DEALER

A bought ledger clerk used a forged driving licence to open a bank account in a name very similar to a supplier. He then prepared one set of payment documentation for a genuine invoice and another for a phoney one. Both were buried in a large pile of authorisation requests. As the accounting system might highlight duplicate payments he ensured that the false cheque request was for £2,000 more than the genuine invoice.

The clerk took a calculated risk that no one would check for inconsistencies between requisitions and invoices. When the cheque had been raised and signed the clerk stole the cheque from the office out-tray where it had been left overnight.

Look out for the following signs.

Cheque stock security:

- cheque-books kept in desk drawers or filing cabinets;
- computer-generated cheques left on a printer;
- poor voiding procedures for unused or spoilt cheques;
- cashiers' offices in open-plan areas or room with no locks;
- no restrictions on access to the cashiers' area; and
- no cheque usage log recording first, last and voided cheques.

Cheque processing:

- poor segregation of duties between key functions, eg ordering and payments;
- cheques still used despite availability of electronic payments;
- payee and amount lines left uncrossed;
- abbreviation of payee details, eg 'IR' for 'Inland Revenue';
- cheques awaiting signature or despatch left on unattended desks; and
- cheques left in trays or unlocked desk drawers/filing cabinets overnight.

Post handling:

- cheques sent in internal mail envelopes or specially coloured transmission wallets;
- cheques sent in semi-transparent or window envelopes;
- envelopes containing cheques left overnight in post baskets; and
- incoming or outgoing post left in bags in vulnerable areas, eg near staff entrances.

Other:

- no clear desk policy: cheques or documents with bank account details and key signatures left lying around;
- poor control over access for contractors' staff;
- poor physical security, especially during building work;

- poor recruitment screening by the company, contractors and agents; and

- no fraud response plan to capture, evaluate and investigate suspicions of fraud or theft.

7.4.2 Electronic payments fraud

Many large electronic payment frauds have occurred because of inadequate fund release procedures. Processing is sometimes carried out by junior staff with final release requiring no more than a check that someone is an authorised signatory.

FINAL PAYMENT

A company ensured that staff leavers be paid outstanding bonus and other accrued benefits but only on the last day of their service. The finance manager in charge of the payments area noticed that reconciliations were often delayed and were usually carried out by junior inexperienced staff. He started making additional payments to a number of leaver names however he included his, rather than the leavers' bank account details in the payment batch.

The lists were authorised and soon he started accumulating a large sum in his personal bank account. The leavers were not aware of the amounts as they were not expecting these additions.

The finance managers' activities were uncovered while he took time off. It turned out that he had been diverting monthly payments for over 10 years.

Look out for the following.

1. Payment devices not kept in locked safes.

2. Passwords written on guidance booklets, by PC screens, etc.

3. Evidence of payments being made without one or both authorised members of staff being involved (even if payments are legitimate).

4. Payee bank accounts sharing the same details with employees' bank accounts.

5. Changes in payee bank account numbers from the previous payment or in the master files.

6. Payee names appearing the same as those of employees and employers.

7. Payee names made out in abbreviated form.

8. Unsegregated duties, eg the same person making payments and undertaking bank reconciliations.

9. Alterations to BACS listings after the original data entry.

10. No management review of bank reconciliations or reviews undertaken in a cursory fashion.

11. An untidy balance sheet with unnecessary credit balances/provisions.

12. Poor budget-holder accountability.

13. Incorrect payments posted to expense accounts.

7.4.3 Manipulation of bank reconciliations and cash books

Bank reconciliations must be properly prepared and subject to periodic, thorough and independent checks. It is alarmingly easy to change formulae on spreadsheets so that a reconciliation appears to balance, despite the item being a fraudulent payment. A number of frauds would have been spotted if reconciliations had been periodically reperformed, eg during enforced holiday absence, and the details checked against other ledgers and supporting documentation.

Other risks include the following.

1. Rolling matching – incorrect matching of reconciliation items in order to conceal a fraud. This is most likely when many items for similar amounts are going through an account.

2. Incorrect description of reconciling items.

3. Incorrect description of items in cash books

4. Use of compensating debits/credits in other ledgers to make the bank reconciliation 'work'.

Look out for these signs.

1. No independent detailed check of bank reconciliations.

2. Different cut-off days for bank and ledger dates.

3. Excessive numbers of contras/adjustments on reconciliations.

4. No review of endorsements or alterations on returned cheques.

5. Bank account details that do not relate to the ledger account being reconciled.

111

7.4.4   Money transfer fraud

This involves external fraudsters making illicit transfers via misuse of passwords and authorisation codes. Staff collusion is a common feature of such crimes.

Look out for:

- transfers to or from offshore accounts or countries with bank secrecy laws;

- transfers to or from individuals who are not regular suppliers;

- abbreviated payee names and alterations to date, amount, payee or other details;

- poor control over documents between approval and processing stages;

- processing of significant transactions by junior personnel;

- poor security for the room where transfer instructions are issued; and

- poor security for codes and passwords.

7.4.5   Forged cheques

This can also involve theft of cheques or cheque-books. Forgeries may be based on cancelled or returned cheques and documents containing authorised signatories, which can also be used to obtain cheque-books from the bank. Fraudsters also scan signatures electronically. Warning signs are those as for misuse of cheques and payment systems.

7.5   Other types of fraud in manufacturing and services

7.5.1   Share support schemes

There are many well-known cases of directors using a company's funds to support its share price. Off-shore companies and other complex structures are used to conceal the identity of the purchaser. 'Consultancy' or other fees may be paid to counterparties to purchase shares.

It is difficult to identify warning signs for all potential schemes. The financial position of the company, its trading performance, recent movements in share prices, stock market conditions and significant proposed transactions, such as a major acquisition are all important. Complex structures, including a pattern of purchases by offshore

112

companies, or transactions which are shrouded in secrecy, should be regarded with suspicion.

7.5.2   Misuse of pension funds or other assets

Pension fund assets have often been misappropriated to bail out ailing companies, eg used as security to obtain loans.

Look out for the following signs.

1. Access to assets created through special legal arrangements, eg powers of attorney, investment management agreements and trustee companies.

2. Different accounting periods for the fund and the company.

3. Transfers of assets between company and pension fund at times when market values are hard to ascertain.

7.5.3   Company car scheme frauds

These usually involve the sale of ex-fleet cars to connected parties at discount prices. External frauds include over-billing for labour on servicing or repairs, particularly where the invoice is passed directly to the employing company along with the company car (so avoiding inspection by the previous user). Agency cards may be misused to purchase fuel or parts for non-company vehicles.

Look out for the following.

1. No independent checks on the prices at which company cars are sold, or to whom they are sold.

2. Same purchaser for a range of models.

3. Single source of supply for essential services such as repairs.

7.5.4   Payroll and pension frauds

Payroll frauds involve the use of dummy employees, unauthorised salary increases, together with bogus commissions, bonuses and overtime payments. The risk is particularly high when duties are poorly segregated and remote locations poorly supervised.

Poor control in pension administration departments paves the way for fraud. In one case a fraudster identified pensioners who had no next of kin. When they died he arranged for ongoing payments to be sent to bank accounts under his control.

113

2. Fraud risk management demands a clear understanding of types of purchases/sales, the nature of suppliers/customers, the form of contracts and how sales/purchases are organised.

3. Many problems can be avoided by the rigorous application of quite basic controls. Failings common to most types of fraud in manufacturing and services include:

   (a) poor segregation of duties;
   (b) failure to verify the credentials of suppliers, customers and referees;
   (c) a lack of independent monitoring of vendor or customer complaints;
   (d) no independent appraisal of pricing and purchasing structures;
   (e) lack of clear internal accountability;
   (f) refusal to query deals which seem 'too good to be true';
   (g) failure to monitor remote locations properly;
   (h) suppliers and customers being dealt with outside the main system and/or by a single manager; and
   (i) leaving cheques and cheque-books on desks or in unlocked filing cabinets.

8 Fraud in the financial sector

Financial services companies are not only susceptible to many of the frauds described in earlier chapters, they are also vulnerable to a large number of more specialised frauds. This chapter discusses these in some detail. While some financial institutions such as retail banks and general insurers generally experience higher levels of external fraud to other organisations all financial institutions are particularly at risk from insider fraud, often by top staff, sometimes in collusion with organised crime. High levels of awareness are vital as fraudulent transactions can give a misleading impression of an institution's financial health.

8.1 Banking

Frauds against banks fall into five main categories.

- insider fraud;
- credit and mortgage fraud;
- deposit taking;
- bank account fraud; and
- dealing fraud.

8.1.1 Insider fraud

Financial institutions are particularly at risk from staff fraud because staff may have access to valuable personal data as well as funds. Staff at these companies are also targets for organised crime when criminals want access to the personal data and the funds of account holders.

8.1.2 Credit

There are four main parts of the lending process:

- introduction and appraisal of borrower;
- taking security and releasing funds;
- maintaining the loan with the false information; and
- payment of interest, repayment of loan principal and release of security.

The most common frauds at each stage of the process are illustrated below.

Figure 8.1 Typical credit frauds

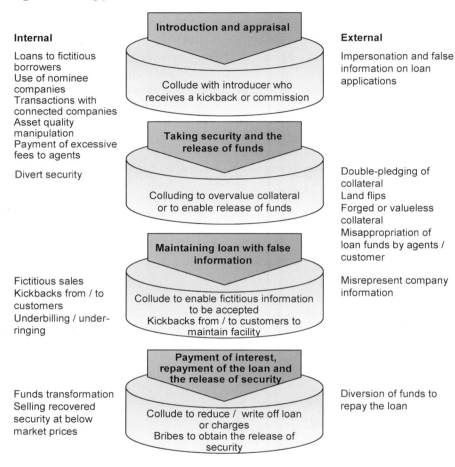

Internal

Loans to fictitious borrowers
Use of nominee companies
Transactions with connected companies
Asset quality manipulation
Payment of excessive fees to agents

Divert security

Fictitious sales
Kickbacks from / to customers
Underbilling / under-ringing

Funds transformation
Selling recovered security at below market prices

External

Impersonation and false information on loan applications

Double-pledging of collateral
Land flips
Forged or valueless collateral
Misappropriation of loan funds by agents / customer

Misrepresent company information

Diversion of funds to repay the loan

Introduction and appraisal
Collude with introducer who receives a kickback or commission

Taking security and the release of funds
Colluding to overvalue collateral or to enable release of funds

Maintaining loan with false information
Collude to enable fictitious information to be accepted
Kickbacks from / to customers to maintain facility

Payment of interest, repayment of the loan and the release of security
Collude to reduce / write off loan or charges
Bribes to obtain the release of security

Introduction and appraisal

Key issues relate to the borrowers' identity and financial status, who introduced them and on what terms. Internal frauds include obtaining loans on the basis of false information, eg by inflating an applicant's income, the creation of fictitious loans and disguised loans to the financial institution's own employees. The latter practice involves the use of nominees, front companies and 'deposit transformation' where the fraudster makes a deposit with a 'friendly' bank, which in turn lends the money to a nominated beneficiary. Management may also approve loans in which they have an undisclosed interest, eg via joint venture or profit-sharing arrangements. The extent of lending is sometimes concealed in order to meet regulatory requirements. Bribery is often a factor in such frauds. External frauds include impersonation and the submission of false information on loan applications.

Taking security and releasing funds

Key concerns relate to the nature and value of the security; ensuring that there is no release of funds before appropriate security is taken; and ensuring that loans are used for the purpose for which they were intended. Internal frauds include using the bank's own funds as loan collateral. External frauds include double pledging of collateral by borrowers, land flips (sales between connected parties to boost valuations artificially), fraudulent valuations, use of forged or valueless collateral, loans used for invalid purposes, and misappropriation of funds by solicitors and agents.

Maintaining loan with false information

The circumstances of the loan recipient may change or false information provided in order to avoid having to repay the loan. Internal frauds include under recording the loan principal value and fictitious sales and external frauds include the provision of misleading information about the company. Collusion between financial institution employee and the customer is aimed at maintaining the line of credit.

Payment of interest, repayment of loan and release of security

The main concerns here are that payments are made, and made in accordance with the loan agreement. Where a payment problem arises management may resort to painting a false picture of the borrower's financial position in order to avoid making provisions to cover regulatory requirements or to avoid a negative impact on performance measures. One method is to use the bank's or depositors' money to make it seem as if the borrower has made a repayment.

Management sometimes transfer problem loans to other parts of the group, where they may be subject to less scrutiny by auditors or regulators. Loans may also be transferred to connected parties with an agreement to repurchase at some future date. External frauds include bribes paid to managers or employees to obtain release of security before a loan is repaid.

Sales of recovered security are often poorly controlled. In one case, a bank credit officer arranged loans to his co-conspirators to purchase assets at prices much below market values.

Specific types of credit and mortgage fraud are set out below.

Loans to fictitious borrowers

Loans are created using false personal details and financial information. Individuals or companies with good credit status also lend their names to those in poor standing so they can obtain loans. This type of fraud is quite common in the retail banking sector where a large number of false loan applications, each for a relatively small amount, may be involved.

GAMBLING HABIT

A branch manager created overdraft facilities for five customers without their consent, forging 200 cheques worth US$59 million to fund his gambling habit. Head office and internal audit made little effort to monitor accounts introduced or handled exclusively by a branch manager. Nor was there any attempt to review the underlying business in significant accounts.

Look out for the following.

1. Thin loan files with sketchy and incomplete financial information or photocopied or scrappy documentation.

2. Loans or overdrafts where management claim the borrower's 'creditworthiness is undoubted' despite poor documentation.

3. Borrowers with common or like-sounding names.

4. Significant number of borrowers introduced by the same source.

5. Borrowers not on the electoral register, with missing credit checks or references or discrepancies that are not followed up.

6. High valuations where the valuers are from outside the usually permitted area or where the same valuer deals with numerous applications.

7. Commercial customers or significant personal borrowers who are not generally known to staff.

8. Funds released before all necessary formalities are completed.

9. Staff remuneration closely linked to the number and/or value of new loans.

10. Generous extensions or revised terms when a borrower defaults.

11. Proportion of problem loans arranged by one lending agent/manager appears disproportionately large.

Use of nominee companies

The fraudster may seek to disguise borrowing through offshore companies or trustee or management arrangements. Files and documentation kept outside the main filing system should be regarded with suspicion. Lack of cooperation with enquiries about particular loans, including difficulties in accessing information, may be a warning sign.

PERSONAL PAPERS

The managing director of a bank made a loan to himself via his own offshore company, though the bank's loan file implied he had merely introduced the business. The file also indicated that the loan was to meet short-term working capital requirements. There was very little information about the company, its directors, activities or financial position. Documents which revealed the true nature of the loan were kept in the managing director's office; there was little to confirm appropriate know your customer (KYC) details.

Look out for the following.

1. Loan files with sketchy or incomplete financial information.

2. Loans to individuals or companies in jurisdictions outside the area of normal operations for the bank/branch.

3. Loans to offshore companies without a clear business purpose.

4. Complex structures shrouded in secrecy.

5. Few details on file about the individuals behind particular companies or loan arrangements.

6. Strong loan recommendation from senior bank officials without much supporting detail.

7. Incomplete or unvalidated KYC documentation.

8. Borrowers with like-sounding names.

9. Customers handled exclusively by one member of staff.

Transactions with connected companies

Though some loans may appear to be to third-party borrowers, these can in fact be linked to joint-venture or profit-sharing arrangements for the benefit of the bank's senior staff.

FALSE FINANCIAL STATEMENTS

Loans amounting to US$236 million were granted to an individual owning several companies. He diverted the money to pay personal expenses and repay other loans. The banks had taken the supporting financial data at face value despite his submitting false financial statements, inventory lists and invoices. There was also poor monitoring of how the funds were used.

Warning signs are the same as those listed under 'Loans to fictitious borrowers' above, but look out for the following.

1. Use of nominee companies.

2. Jottings on a file inconsistent with the other information it contains, eg names, addresses and telephone numbers of unknown individuals.

3. Repayments made by persons other than the borrower.

Asset quality manipulation

Managers may need to conceal the extent of lending to particular borrowers, either to avoid provisions or to meet regulatory requirements. Such manipulation is designed to artificially enhance the apparent quality of assets.

LARGE EXPOSURES

A bank chief executive agreed that finance for a series of large overseas projects should be spread between several offshore companies. Ownership was disguised to conceal from the bank's auditors and the regulator the true extent of the borrowing. Some projects ran into difficulties, but the complex structure enabled advances to be made in respect of apparently new, unconnected ventures which were in fact designed to meet loan repayments.

Warning signs are the same as for use of nominee companies.

Kickback, inducements and commissions

The details required to obtain a loan may be falsified, or borrowers may bribe staff in order to obtain credit or manipulate lending criteria. The risk of this type of fraud is increased where loan officer remuneration is linked to the volume and/or value of new loans that he or she makes. Unwise lending may also be approved at the end of bonus assessment periods in order to earn commissions.

LENDING LIMIT

A lending agent encouraged customers to inflate their income so they could take out higher mortgages. Had their actual earnings been known the company might not have lent so much and the agent's commission would have been reduced.

Look out for:

*   excessive amounts of business generated by particular loan officers;

*   lending criteria overridden regularly by particular loan officers;

- customers with only one bank contact; and

- customer details which cannot be independently certified.

Use of parallel organisations

Parallel organisations are companies under the covert control of a bank's directors and/or shareholders. They are often used in asset quality manipulation and funds transformation (see below), undisclosed sale and repurchase agreements, circular refinancing arrangements and sales at other than market value.

Parallel organisations may also be used to ostensibly secure a bank's lending. Bank funds are transferred to an offshore company masquerading as a third-party depositor who uses them as supposed cash collateral for the loan.

Pressing personal needs

A bank made a short-term loan to meet 'pressing personal needs', secured by a cash deposit from an offshore company. The borrower was a friend of the bank's managing director who in turn owned the offshore company. Funds transferred were drawn from other customers' long-term deposit accounts or under hold-mail arrangements.

Look out for the following.

1. Unexpected settlement of problem loans shortly before the period end or prior to an audit visit.

2. Unexpected new lending close to the period end.

3. Transfers of loans, especially to companies which are suspected of having some connection with the directors and/or shareholders.

4. Poor controls over the giving and recording of guarantees or similar commitments.

5. Transactions or structures shrouded in secrecy.

6. Changes in patterns of business with related organisations.

Funds transformation

When a borrower seems likely to default on a loan, management may seek to give a false impression of his financial soundness in order to avoid making provisions or to satisfy regulatory requirements. 'Funds transformation' involves concealment of the nature or source of funds. Sometimes the loans involved may be connected with the directors or staff of the bank or set up for some fraudulent purpose.

123

ROUND THE HOUSES

A bank made a loan to purchase a property development undertaken by the chairman's brother-in-law. The loan was non-performing and there was a shortfall on the security. The bank transferred an amount equal to the shortfall through a branch, a subsidiary and an associated institution under its management and back to the bank as though it were a receipt from the chairman's brother-in-law.

Look out for the following.

1. Sources of receipt inconsistent with standing data.

2. Unclear business purposes for transactions with companies in, or associated with, the same group.

3. Arrangements involving offshore companies and/or companies under common ownership.

4. Annotations on file which do not appear to relate to the borrower, eg names, addresses and telephone numbers.

5. Files kept outside the normal areas.

Selling recovered security at below market prices

Many banks have strong credit procedures and controls for the main part of the credit cycle. But these can be much less rigorous where the borrower has defaulted and the bank is in possession of the recovered security. Checking of prices at which such assets are sold, and the parties to whom they are sold, are sometimes very weak, creating opportunities for bank officers to obtain hidden profits or kickbacks.

Bribes to obtain release of security or reduce amount claimed

This applies to release of security before the loan principal has been repaid, and to reducing the bank's claims when a loan is in default.

Impersonation

Impersonation and the submission of false information on loan applications are significant threats for any bank, particularly those with inexperienced loan officers or which only provide for desk-top reviews. Vulnerability is especially high during periods of rapid growth when banks are vying to gain market share.

A crucial part of the loan appraisal stage is assessing the person who has introduced the business and how well he knows the borrower. An introducer or broker may simply want to develop a stronger business relationship and have no great knowledge of the loan applicant. It is also important to look for concentrations of business originating from individual introducers, eg loan brokers, and possible connections between them and bank staff.

Look out for the following signs.

1. Grandiose but uncorroborated claims on purported volumes of business, particularly where it is hard to validate information, ie if the valuer has operated in another location.

2. Extravagant lifestyle of the introducer or lavish entertaining of bank officials.

3. No appraisal of the borrower at his own business premises.

4. Business ventures that appear too good to be true.

5. Inexperienced loan officers.

6. Customers with only one bank contact.

7. Difficulty in corroborating credentials, inconsistent or missing documentation and inconsistencies in personal details, eg electoral registration and credit status.

False financial information

All manner of information can be falsified at any time, including details relating to the nature of the underlying business or contract, returns, financial statements, supporting sales invoices and other vouchers.

DUMMY SALES INVOICES

A corporate borrower hired mechanical plant to local authorities and contractors. The company ran into financial problems, partly due to rapid expansion. The director submitted copies of false invoices to a bank which advanced 70 per cent of their value. These were for work in areas not covered by the local authorities and on roads which did not exist. The fraud came to light when discrepancies were discovered.

Look out for the following.

1. 'Scrappy' documentation.

2. Inconsistencies within or between documents.

3. Documents supposedly from different sources using same typeface/paper.

4. Delays in obtaining documents.

5. Missing information, eg VAT numbers on invoices.

6. Evasive replies/lack of knowledge when questions are asked about documentary evidence.

Double pledging of collateral, land flips and valueless collateral

Many external frauds against banks involve the use of false or misvalued security: the double pledging of collateral, forged or valueless collateral or collateral whose value has been inflated. The latter often involves what are known as 'land flips' – sales of property between connected parties to artificially boost the valuation of the property (there is usually a series of such sales). There can also be bribes to obtain false valuations and certifications.

Risks are greatly increased where bank staff fail to make site visits. In one case this would have exposed the fact that refurbishment work was of a much lower quality than indicated in the loan application.

Look out for the following.

1. Valuer coming from outside the area where the property is situated.
2. Same valuer used in a large number of transactions, or by both parties.
3. Series of sales of a particular asset over a short period with values increasing on each sale.
4. Identity of principals difficult to ascertain/use of nominee or 'front' companies.
5. Borrower having access to substantial assets which are similar to those pledged.

Misappropriation of loan funds by agents/customers

The warning signs here are as for impersonation and false information on loan applications.

A BRIDGE TOO FAR

A solicitor obtained over £250,000 from a bank by pretending the money would go to clients who were planning to buy property. He got the clients to sign blank forms in case bridging loans were needed quickly. He also had an arrangement with the bank that when bridging loans were required the money would be transferred into his company's account. The money was used instead to top up his company's resources and to fund exotic holidays and lavish entertaining.

This and a number of the other types of scenarios, where funds are provided as a result of false information, may have regulatory ramifications. In the UK the Proceeds of Crime Act 2002, Part 7 requires suspicions to be reported to the Serious Organised Crime Agency. The law requires reporting of suspected or actual laundering of the proceeds of crime and there are penalties for individuals who fail to do so. While reporting applies mainly to businesses in UK regulated sectors such as banks and accountants, the provisions of the Act (such as concealing or transferring criminal property) go wider. Appropriate advice should be obtained to ensure management and staff understand their obligations under the Act.

Diversion of funds to repay loan

Sometimes borrowers decide that they have a better use for funds than repaying a loan.

FRAUDULENT FACTORING

A bank granted factoring facilities of £4 million to two companies under common ownership. But the directors failed to tell customers that debts should be paid directly to the bank and their payments were used as working capital to keep both companies afloat. The directors also submitted bogus invoices to the bank. When the facilities came up for renewal £2 million was outstanding and the companies subsequently went into liquidation.

8.1.3 Deposit fraud

The deposit-taking cycle falls into three key phases:

1. Verifying the identity of the depositor and establishing the source of funds.

2. Recording the funds deposited.

3. Handling the funds in accordance with the customer's instructions.

Verifying the identity of new customers and establishing the source of the funds

Verifying the identity of new customers and establishing the source of the funds deposited are key requirements for any bank. The main concern is money laundering. Though this is beyond the scope of this book, it is worth pointing out that customer verification should not only apply to new customers. Existing accounts, particularly for organisations, should be continually monitored to ensure awareness of changes in ownership or management. There is also a risk that managers and staff may collude with depositors to disguise the latter's identity, eg by using code names.

Recording of funds deposited

A number of international banking frauds have involved diversion of deposits to fraudster-controlled accounts and the deposits not being

127

Figure 8.2 Typical depositor frauds

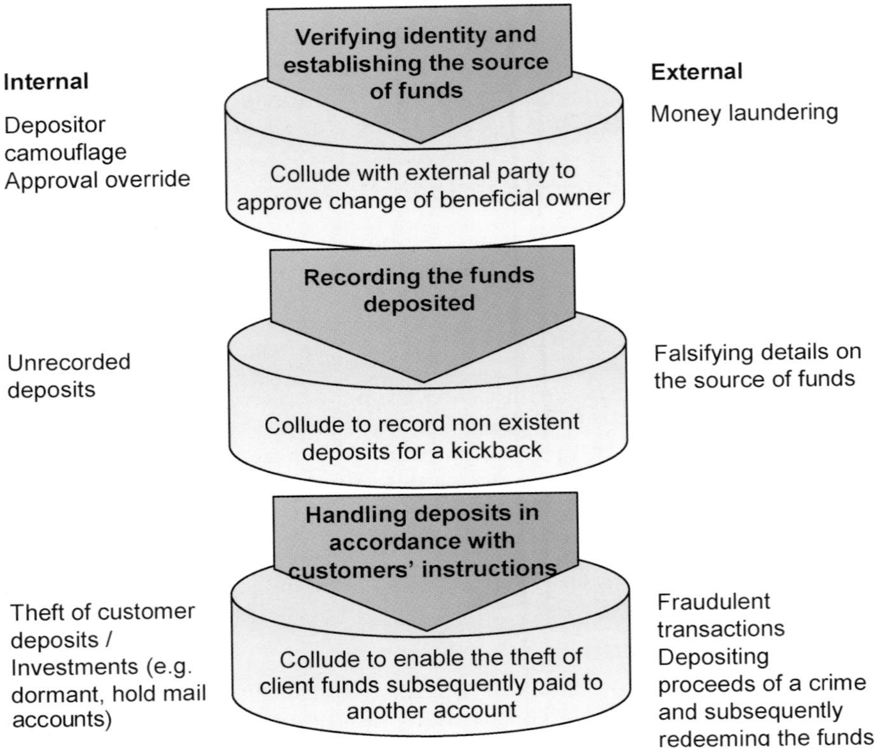

Internal

Depositor
camouflage
Approval override

Verifying identity and establishing the source of funds

Collude with external party to approve change of beneficial owner

External

Money laundering

Unrecorded
deposits

Recording the funds deposited

Collude to record non existent deposits for a kickback

Falsifying details on
the source of funds

Theft of customer
deposits /
Investments (e.g.
dormant, hold mail
accounts)

Handling deposits in accordance with customers' instructions

Collude to enable the theft of client funds subsequently paid to another account

Fraudulent
transactions
Depositing
proceeds of a crime
and subsequently
redeeming the funds

recorded in the bank's books. Banks operating hold-mail arrangements are particularly susceptible to this type of fraud, as are those taking long-term deposits from overseas customers with whom they are rarely in contact.

Handling deposits in accordance with the customers' instructions

The key issues relate to proper segregation of the customers' funds and ensuring that transfers from deposit accounts, or sales of customer investments, are made in accordance with properly authorised instructions. Internal frauds involve the merging of depositor and personal funds and the theft of customer funds or investments. External frauds include the use of fraudulent payment instructions.

Depositors' camouflage

As noted above, management may collude with a depositor to conceal the depositor's identity via false names. A large number of such names may be used. Managers may also set up disguised accounts to conceal their interests and criminally acquired funds. A bank may conceal the extent to which its deposit base derives from a particular source, or that depositors are in fact directors or their associates.

Look out for the following.

1. Similar or like-sounding names across various accounts.

2. Offshore corporate depositors with no clearly defined business or which supply few details.

3. Depositor files containing little information, particularly where customers live in countries associated with drug trafficking or terrorist activities.

Unrecorded deposits

A number of major international banking frauds have involved the diversion of deposits to fraudster-controlled accounts. The funds are often not recorded in the bank's books. Deposits are routed through intermediaries or receipts paid away by the bank. Transactions are not recorded. Accounts to which funds are diverted are often located in offshore locations.

This type of fraud is most likely to occur where depositors are resident overseas and/or where funds are held on long-term deposit or under hold-mail arrangements. As a result the customer may not be in regular contact with the bank or receive statements. The risk is increased where depositors have removed funds from an oppressive home jurisdiction and therefore place more trust in their new bank.

Theft of customer deposits/investments

The scope for fraud is increased where (as above) customers are not in regular contact with their bankers or give them considerable discretion.

Look out for the following.

1. Customers with hold-mail arrangements having only occasional contact with the bank.

2. No independent resolution of customer complaints or review of hold-mail accounts.

3. Transactions made without appropriate support or instructions.

Fraudulent instructions

Cases involving false instructions are considered in section 8.3.7.

8.1.4 Bank account fraud

This can be instigated internally or externally. 'Account takeover' is a typical variation. A high value or dormant customer's account is targeted after the fraudster has located it by obtaining information via corruption, mail theft, combing household rubbish, etc. He then transfers the funds to an account under his control and withdraws them.

8.1.5 Confidential data loss

Details of a bank customer's name, address, date of birth, employment, family relationships, etc. are gold dust to fraudsters. The following actions will help keep such data safe.

1. Encourage staff, customers and other relevant parties to raise suspicions with the nominated person(s) in the firm.

2. Make internal reporting channels clear and confidential.

3. Ensure continuous staff education and awareness raising about data protection.

4. Enhance transaction-monitoring arrangements.

5. Request customers to present proof of identity whenever suspicions are raised.

6. Establish robust data-loss risk assessment and follow up with risk mitigation programmes.

8.1.6 Dealing fraud

Dealing fraud falls into two categories.

1. Misappropriation, whereby a dealer takes funds, either directly or indirectly, for his own purposes.

2. False reporting/accounting, whereby a dealer misrepresents the financial performance of an area under his control. This may not entail direct loss but will always involve unauthorised activity and can give a misleading impression of the institutions' financial health.

There are four main motives for dealing fraud.

1. Direct personal benefit – the dealer siphons off cash for his own use.

2. Job protection – the dealer incurs a loss, often by mistake, and uses fraudulent transactions to hide it and protect his position. Another course is to not mark or adjust his position to reflect the market price.

3. Increased remuneration – a common method is to undertake a

dishonest transaction in order to inflate reported profits. Profits in a dealer's book are often related to bonus payments.

4. Something for a rainy day – rather than recognising an exceptional profit the dealer hides some of it for release when trading is down.

Some of the more notable dealing frauds have involved 'downward spirals'. A dealer incurs but does not report a loss or reports a false profit. He must then generate a real profit to cover the loss and so increases his position. The loss grows if the market moves against him and the spiral continues until it becomes hard to disguise.

The impact of the 2007/08 'sub prime' crisis or 'credit crisis' has also had an impact on the dealing operations of a number of financial institutions. Volatile equity or stock prices have also affected the value of their asset holdings. Dealers may be required to mark their book to market and a dramatic fall in prices is likely to reduce performance, thus impacting on their bonuses and remuneration.

It is once again instructive to consider the fraud triangle. Poor controls create opportunity. Appropriate monitoring and robust challenge of dealing operations is essential but will not be effective if those charged with oversight do not understand the intricacies of dealing. Bonuses provide motivation and dealers could seek to rationalise fraudulent acts if they believe there is a low risk of being caught and that manipulation is an acceptable if covert practice.

Dealer enters into the deal

When the dealer enters into the deal the key issues are the price at which it is struck and his relationship with the counter-party. Frauds involve the use of false market prices, eg through off-market rings or related-party deals. Concentrations of business with particular brokers can indicate that the dealer is receiving a payment from a broker in return for his business. Concentration can also indicate churning, whereby the dealer and/or counterparty dealer receive additional remuneration from dealing activity.

Deal slip is completed

When the deal slip is completed and entered into the accounting system it must be properly recorded on a timely basis. Dealers may suppress information to hide loss-making transactions, or delay their input to appear to keep within prescribed limits. They may manipulate profits between client accounts and the firm's own portfolio. Dealers may input fictitious transactions to avoid showing a loss or recognise a profit, and to disguise a position. Unnecessary suspense accounts are often used by fraudsters to cover their tracks and should be closed.

Figure 8.3 Typical dealing frauds

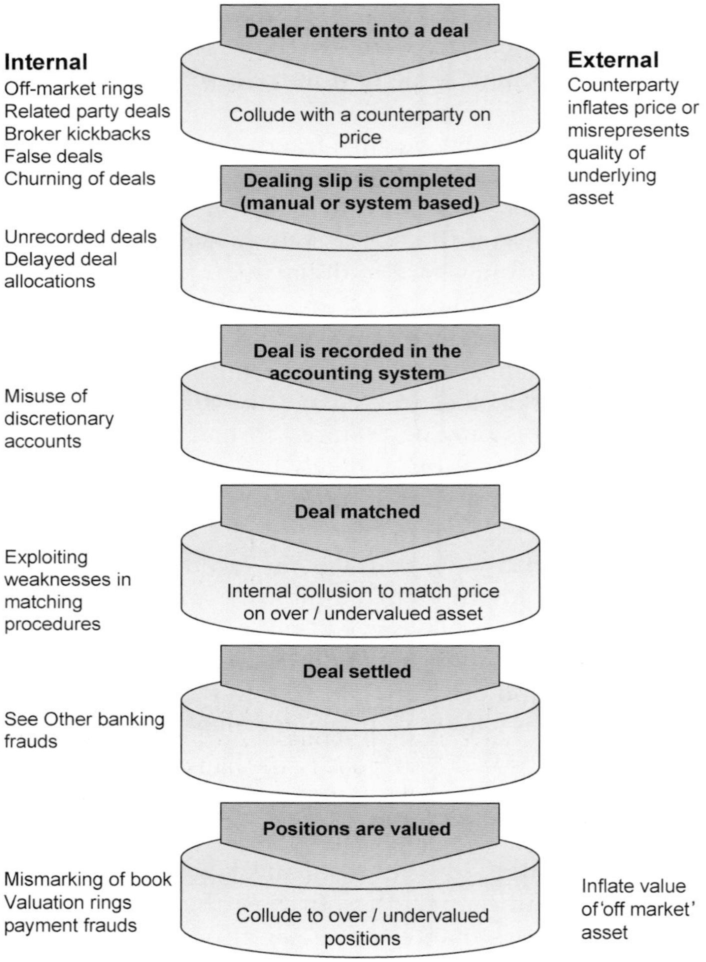

Dealer enters into a deal

Internal
Off-market rings
Related party deals
Broker kickbacks
False deals
Churning of deals

Collude with a counterparty on price

External
Counterparty
inflates price or
misrepresents
quality of
underlying
asset

Unrecorded deals
Delayed deal
allocations

Dealing slip is completed (manual or system based)

Misuse of
discretionary
accounts

Deal is recorded in the accounting system

Exploiting
weaknesses in
matching
procedures

Deal matched

Internal collusion to match price on over / undervalued asset

See Other banking
frauds

Deal settled

Mismarking of book
Valuation rings
payment frauds

Positions are valued

Collude to over / undervalued positions

Inflate value
of 'off market'
asset

Deal matching

Opportunities for fraud may arise where deal matching procedures are weak or where there are known loopholes in computerised matching procedures.

Settlement stage

A key factor in many frauds is that deals roll up without settlement. Certain contracts, eg those for forward foreign exchange, do not require immediate settlement. Instruments of this kind are vulnerable to fraud, and losses of hundreds of millions of pounds have been accumulated and concealed.

Valuation

While many financial investments have deep and liquid markets other financial products, particularly derivatives, pose significant valuation challenges. Over-marking a book may lead to bonuses being paid on false profits.

Off-market rings

These involve two or more parties dealing at off-market prices. This may be difficult to spot unless an institution marks its positions to market each day and performs spot checks on the prices at which deals are transacted (there may be problems with this in less liquid markets).

EVERYONE SEEMS TO BE MAKING A PROFIT

A dealer bought a security at 100. He then sold this to an investor at 101 apparently making a profit. In fact the market price was 103 and the investor then sold the shares at that price to another institution which in turn sold them on, at a small profit, to the company employing the dealer. Part of the investor's profit was paid to the dealer as a kickback.

FALSE MARKET IN BOND WARRANTS

A trader bought Swiss franc-dominated put warrants which gave him the right to buy Spanish government bonds. He drove the price of the warrants higher and then sold them back to the bank. He made a profit of £2 million on the deal which he placed in a Swiss bank account. The compliance department picked the trade up and the funds were returned with interest.

Look out for:

- the dealing book not being marked to market on a daily basis;

- no spot checks on prices at which deals are transacted;

- unusual levels of activity with particular counterparties; and

- poor supervision in the dealing room.

Related-party deals

This is when party deals are undertaken at off-market prices with counterparties with whom the institution or dealer has a relationship, the goal being to manipulate profits. Sometimes securities are sold with an undisclosed commitment to buy them back at a later date, perhaps after the year-end audit is complete. Such frauds can be highly complex and succeed because the unrelated parties do not fully understand the product. Warning signs are as for off-market rings.

Broker kickbacks

A significant volume of transactions in the London markets are dealt through brokers rather than between counterparties. Brokers earn a commission on the transactions they arrange. In some cases commissions may be paid to increase the flow of deals through a particular broker. Such arrangements are difficult to identify.

Look out for the following.

1. High levels of business with a particular broker.

2. Unusual trends in broker commissions.

3. Trades in the same security which are then sold and repurchased on several occasions within a short time.

False deals

Dealers may input fictitious transactions to avoid showing a loss, recognise a profit or disguise a position. Poor deal-matching procedures significantly increase the risk of these remaining undetected.

FALSE HEDGES

A trader was instructed not to take more than £2 million of unprotected positions in the Mexican peso. He failed to hedge and acquired an unauthorised position worth over US$200 million. The bank lost about $70 million when the peso was devalued. The trader then entered fictitious transactions to make it appear he had hedged his position and was showing a profit. If the bank had not discovered the fraud the trader would have earned a 125 per cent bonus.

Look out for the following.

1. Unusual trends in dealers' positions.

2. Very high gross compared to net positions.

3. Significant number of unmatched or unconfirmed deals in particular dealing books or with particular counterparties.

4. A significant number of cancelled deals.

5. Unusually high value of unsettled transactions.

Unrecorded deals

A dealer may want to delay inputting his deals to conceal loss-making transactions or hide breaches of dealing limits (which can be a sackable offence).

NO QUESTIONS ASKED

A highly successful foreign-exchange dealer (whose remuneration was linked closely to his profits) used to take unauthorised overnight positions in forward contracts. He booked the unauthorised deals the following day and then booked others reversing the positions.

On one occasion the markets in New York and Tokyo moved against him overnight. He assumed the trend would continue and doubled up his position. But the market reversed.

The unauthorised activity was not discovered because the back office focused almost exclusively on checking settlement date details and ignored trade dates. Details relating to forward deals were only checked on the settlement date.

No questions were asked about how the dealer managed to achieve a high level of profits despite an official strategy which permitted very limited overnight positions.

Look out for:

- high levels of profit by particular dealers in relation to the stated dealing strategy;

- dealing books trading close to their dealing limits;

- unusual trends in dealers' positions; and

- a significant number of unmatched counterparty confirmations.

Delayed deal allocation

Dealers in institutions which trade on their own account as well as for clients may deliberately delay deal allocation while awaiting market movements. This type of fraud can operate in several ways with profitable deals being allocated to the institution itself or to clients who will reimburse the dealer for his efforts, while the less profitable or loss making deals are allocated to other clients.

HEADS I WIN, TAILS I WIN

A bank's head of foreign exchange helped an investor earn 'profits' of approximately £500,000. Transaction details were recorded on the dealer's trading sheet in pencil and later overwritten in ink, replacing speculative figures with actual results.

Look out for the following.

1. No time stamping of deal tickets or review of booking time.

2. Alterations to/overwriting of details on deal sheets.

3. Abnormal profits or losses by particular dealers and their clients.

4. No process to determine whether price allocation has been made on an appropriate basis, particularly on the same stock which has been purchased at various prices throughout the day, to client accounts.

Misuse of discretionary accounts

In the hands of experienced dealers discretionary accounts can be used to hide profits or losses and manipulate results for the period required.

The risk is increased where account statements are not despatched by personnel independent of the dealing room. Poor-quality statements can also conceal the nature and extent of a client's exposure. The risk is heightened if clients fail to check their statements closely (often the case if they appear to be making profits). It is essential to question abnormal profit levels achieved by individual dealers on particular client accounts when these are out of line with the agreed dealing strategy.

Look out for:

*   unusual trends on particular discretionary accounts;

*   clients with only one internal contact;

*   non-standard postings or adjustments to particular accounts; and

*   special arrangements for preparation and issue of statements.

Exploiting weaknesses in deal-matching procedures

Rigorous deal-matching procedures are crucial in any dealing system. Every detail should be agreed with the counterparty as soon as possible. It is difficult to identify warning signs for this particular type of fraud but delays in confirmation are worth further review. If staff place unquestioning reliance on a computer-matching process the problem may go undetected for a considerable period.

> **A GAP IN THE PROGRAM**
>
> The computer for a foreign exchange dealing operation would only process transactions where all specified fields matched with the counterparty's details. Due to a programming error it failed to compare trade date details. Dealers became aware of this loophole which allowed them to misrepresent positions by recording them on days other than actual trade dates.

Mismarking the book

One of the more difficult areas in a dealing portfolio is determining market values at the end of reporting periods. If markets for particular instruments are thin, or if pricing arrangements are complex, there is considerable scope for dealers to misvalue positions in order to hit targets.

The tremendous growth in over-the-counter products (particularly derivatives) has provided great scope for such misvaluation. Institutions most at risk are those with a gap between the skills and experience of front and middle, or back-office, personnel.

Some newer products have no clear market price and a misvaluation by only a few points can have a significant impact on reported profits for a large book. Independent review and testing of the prices used for profit reporting is essential for any institution with a significant number of over-the-counter and derivative products.

Look out for:

- no detailed valuation policies and guidelines;
- pace of new product launches getting out of line with systems development; and
- unusual trends in particular book values.

Valuation rings

Position values are often checked by comparing revaluation prices with third-party sources. In certain cases a dealer may have agreed with a third party (another dealer or a trader in a corporate treasury) to supply non-market prices when information is requested.

8.2   Other banking frauds

8.2.1   Fictitious borrowers/false information on mortgage applications

This is a particular threat when building societies and banks are fighting to gain a bigger share of a rising market. It is common for lending criteria to be poorly devised and applied and there is often a shortage of staff with the right skills and experience.

Though the individual making the loan or mortgage application may be the one named on the form, some or all of the other details may be false. In some cases the applicant not only lies to obtain the loan, he makes a number of payments before defaulting, supposedly due to a decline in his financial circumstances. The lender then repossesses the property and, having recovered its funds, pays any remaining balance to the

137

Look out for:

- unusual terms of business; and

- journals and adjustments posted to volume accounts but inadequately explained.

8.2.7 Cross-firing (or cheque kiting)

Cross-firing involves the accumulation of balances from uncollected cheques drawn on similar accounts at other banks. The fraudster simply takes advantage of delays in the banking system. It is common for a number of accounts to be used.

Look out for:

- a number of deposits with similar and/or round-sum amounts;

- high proportion of regular transactions undertaken with another bank;

- early withdrawal of deposits;

- flow through accounts with no apparent business rationale; and

- accounts with low average balances but high transaction volumes.

KITING

A fraudster opened accounts at two banks. He would draw a cheque against his account at one of the banks (Bank 1) and deposit it in his account at the other bank (Bank 2).

He would then write out a cheque from his account at Bank 2, based on the nominal but uncleared funds and deposit it in Bank 1. Shortly after, he then wrote out a cheque from his account at Bank 1 and deposited it in his account at Bank 2, repeating this process over the following months. He was caught some months later after a cheque he wrote to an external party failed to clear and one of the banks reviewed the account's activity. He had at the time written out cheques for over $200,000 despite originally having a low cash deposit.

8.2.8 Cheque fraud

Cheque fraud includes impersonation, false personal details, altering payee details, forging signatures and manufacturing copies of company cheques. It can occur to both incoming (receivable) and outgoing (payable) cheques.

NEAR-PERFECT COPIES

Four individuals made near-perfect copies of stolen blank cheques on a stolen laser photocopier. They paid them into bank accounts under false names before withdrawing money from cash points. Over six months they printed £100,000-worth of cheques in a lock-up garage and cashed nearly half of them (as well as stealing £60,000 in a series of thefts and burglaries). The photocopies were so accurate that only forensic tests distinguished them from the real thing.

Look out for:

- alterations to cheques;

- illegible signatures;

- printing inconsistencies;

- customers resident outside the normal trading area of the branch or bank;

- applicant in a hurry to open an account or displaying unusual behaviour; and

- inconsistencies arising from credit status and other checks.

INFLATED VALUES

A company's cheques were diverted by an accounts receivable clerk prior to being recorded in the system. He then took the stolen cheques at the end of the day and gave them to his crime masters. Payee and amount details were changed and significantly higher values were recorded on the cheques. In one case, a company paying its account had the value of its cheque increased from less than $200 to $25,000.

Customer complaints spurred the company into action. A shadow investigation identified a number of cheques being excluded from batches created in accounts receivable. The culprit was caught red-handed, leaving with a number of customer cheques in his pocket.

8.2.9 Electronic payment fraud

Some of the largest frauds have involved misuse of money transfer systems. Many are discovered by chance rather than through effective controls. They require no more than changing the details of a receiving account.

In order to combat this risk companies should ensure that staff access is usually confined to the text files containing the data, and that changes cannot be made after proper payment authorisation has been given.

THE POWER OF DETAIL

A 23-year-old clerk had an aptitude for computers and had helped set up a system at his bank. This enabled him to make large transfers to a Swiss bank using his own password plus another stolen from a colleague. He was only caught because he did not know that there was a £19 million limit on cash transfers and because he put a wrong VAT figure on the advice. When the money arrived in Zurich the alarm was raised before it could be sent to a bogus account. The clerk claimed he had been recruited by a gang of international fraudsters and was too frightened to back out. He had been promised £4 million for his part in the crime. When the bank's computer logs were checked it was discovered that he had made three previous abortive attempts.

FORGED LETTERS OF AUTHORITY

A gang of fraudsters telephoned target companies on the pretence of buying a product and suggested payment through the electronic payment system. Armed with the company's account details, they forged corporate letterheads and directors' signatures, instructing the companies' banks to make payments to accounts held by accomplices who were then given a share of the proceeds. Monies were removed before the alarm was raised. The gang attempted 131 such frauds, 33 of which were successful, netting just under £2 million. The fraud was picked up by following a trail of false documents all of which misspelt the word 'sincerely'.

Look out for the following.

1. Insufficient controls over final release of funds relative to the amounts involved, eg checking only that the signatory is an authorised person.

2. Transfers to or from accounts in offshore locations/countries with bank secrecy laws.

3. Transfers to or from individuals who are not regular customers.

4. Abbreviated payee names or instructions and alterations to date, amount, payee or other details.

5. Poor control of documents between approval and processing.

6. Significant transactions processed by junior personnel.

7. Poor security for places where transfers are made and/or over codes and passwords.

8.3 Investment fraud

Investment frauds usually involve a complex web of deceit including false accounting records and bogus documentation. They may be perpetrated by anyone with access to inside information: officers of the company, dealers in the companies' shares, merchant bankers and other advisers.

8.3.1 Selling or lending client investments without authority

This includes surrendering endowment policies and single premium bonds and investment bonds without consent. Client securities can be used as collateral to secure a fraudster's liabilities, which can then be represented as stock 'lent' by the client.

> **SIMPLE BUT EXPENSIVE**
>
> A life insurance agent identified policyholders who had ceased to pay their premiums. He then forged their signatures on policy surrender documents, sending them to head office with a request that the cheques be sent back to him for delivery. He forged endorsements and banked the cheques.

Look out for the following.

1. Abnormal levels of client sales or policy surrenders in relation to the stated investment strategy, or unexpected departures from the strategy.

2. Missing documentation, eg letters of authority.

3. Unusual requests on client files such as a change of address around the time of a balance or payment request.

8.3.2 Share ramping

This involves financial advisers, company executives or others buying substantial amounts of a company's shares at inflated prices in order to give a false impression of their value. Similar frauds may occur via e-mail and on internet news groups tipping 'penny' or other low-value or obscure shares.

Look out for the following.

1. Abnormal increases in the prices of shares of businesses for which the financial advisory company acts as adviser or sponsor.

2. Loans or transactions with no clear commercial purpose.

3. Complex structures/transactions with offshore or 'front' companies.

8.3.3 Front running

Dealers may make profits by undertaking their own transactions rather than those they are paid for. This may be difficult to detect without detailed transaction analysis. The absence of strict rules on, and monitoring of, own account dealings naturally increases the risk of this type of fraud.

8.3.4 Boiler-room scams

These usually involve a group telephoning or e-mailing individuals to get them to buy shares, often in an illiquid market. Investors should be wary of receiving calls from unknown brokers or sellers offering very high returns for products where there is little verifiable information on either product or performance.

8.3.5 Churning

Churning involves the excessive buying and selling of securities in order to generate commission. It usually occurs where a broker is acting in a discretionary capacity, or as investment manager for a particular client.

Look out for the following.

1. Unusually high levels of activity on behalf of particular clients, or high commission levels for particular clients or brokers.

2. Apparent departures from agreed investment strategy.

3. Clients who are rarely in contact with their brokers, eg because the clients are abroad for long periods.

8.3.6 Bogus documents/stolen share certificates

Most investment businesses take good care of share certificates, bearer documents and other valuable assets in their custody. Yet frauds in this area are surprisingly common.

STOLEN PROPERTY

Three individuals defrauded banks, stockbrokers and financial institutions of £12.5 million by inducing them to accept share certificates which had in fact been stolen from a major securities house. They had also tried to sell them through other brokers and to raise loans using the certificates as security.

Look out for the following.

1. Weaknesses in physical security.

2. Overdue reconciliations of custody records with securities held on the premises or at other depositaries.

3. Significant numbers of items on reconciliations which cannot be explained.

4. Insufficient resources/inexperienced staff allocated to monitoring and ensuring that appropriate controls are in place for custody of assets and related records.

8.3.7 Fraudulent instructions

These include forged signatures on share transfer forms, forged power of attorney, bogus fax numbers and email addresses plus unauthorised use of codes and passwords for electronic transfer. The risk is increased where significant transactions are undertaken without contacting the customer directly, or where there is poor code and password security.

Look out for the following.

1. Instructions out of line with clients' usual activities.

2. Abnormal haste in completing a transaction.

3. Unusual aspects in documentation, eg small differences in letter-heads, paper used, typescript, handwriting or postmarks.

8.4 Insurance fraud

A number of the frauds discussed in this section are similar to those discussed elsewhere in this book. But it is still useful to look at them in the context of the insurance industry.

8.4.1 Bogus policies

These include insurance products sold as capital investment bonds, false cover notes, the manipulation of risk classes by agents and fake insurance policies per se.

THE NON-EXISTENT INSURANCE COMPANY

Four individuals collected premiums on commercial liability policies, performance bonds and financial guarantees for building contractors. They issued policies (through an insurance agent where one of them worked) in the name of a non-existent insurance company supposedly incorporated in Anguilla. They gave potential customers and agents false financial statements 'showing' that the company had substantial assets with which to meet claims.

8.4.2 Persuading customers to cancel policies against their interests

This type of fraud enables insurance companies or their agents to generate fraudulent commissions.

Look out for:

- abnormal levels of early policy surrenders; and

- unusual trends in commissions.

8.4.3 Forged surrender of policies or claims

This often occurs where policies have become dormant. The agent forges surrender documentation and pockets the proceeds himself.

8.4.4 Misappropriation of funds

This can occur in a large number of situations, eg by diverting funds provided for investment, or when insurance company employees submit fictitious claims relating to non-existent dependants of eligible policyholders.

A CASE FOR COMPENSATION

A life insurance salesman defrauded 400 investors of their life savings. He accepted monies and arranged for monthly incomes to be paid while misappropriating the larger part of the funds invested. The insurance company did not admit legal responsibility but paid substantial compensation to the victims.

Look out for:

- unusual trends in commissions earned by particular salesmen;

- no independent spot checking of information on claim forms; and

- customer complaints and general correspondence not being independently monitored.

9.2 The role of the internet

The internet has made it profitable for organised criminals to move into large-scale fraud (as already seen in chapter 5). From their point of view it has three great advantages.

9.2.1 Access

The internet allows gangs to attack multiple targets without even entering their premises, often from another jurisdiction. The open systems and networks which boost e-commerce further increase the risk of hacking and illegal access.

9.2.2 Empowerment

The internet allows gang members to associate with less risk and link up with hackers who can supply tools for computer-based fraud. Indeed, hundreds of illicit websites provide regularly updated information and software, often for free. The immense growth in the processing power of PCs and mobile devices such as BlackBerries©, PDAs and smart phones makes it easier to steal data.

9.2.3 Concealment

Routing of transactions through multiple servers, anonymised e-mail accounts, data encryption and proxy computers helps avoid detection and prosecution and also makes recovery action more difficult.

9.3 Public sector fraud

Fraud against the public purse (known as 'fiscal fraud') affects everyone as lost revenue is reflected in higher taxes and poorer public services. Official estimates are that the British welfare system alone loses £50–£100 million a year to organised fraud. In November 2005 the UK's entire online tax credits claim system had to be shut down to stop abuse by gangs of fraudsters. Before 2004, the main fraud threat to this programme was from individuals making false or inflated claims. Organised attacks then mounted rapidly. Theft of personal information, often in bulk from payroll data, enabled criminal organisations to make multiple fraudulent online claims. In one case 50 purported tax agents were used to make 14,000 false returns for a total of £34 million. The National Audit Office estimated total losses from fraud and error to be around £460 million.

The most serious single instance affecting the British public sector is Missing Trader Intra-Community Fraud (MTIC). The loss to public funds in the UK has been estimated at between £2 billion and £5 billion a year. MTIC exploits the free movement of goods between Member States of the European Union by claiming VAT rebates for goods supposedly sold in the British market. It can involve many companies in a chain known as a 'carousel'. A UK trader purchases VAT-free goods, sells them via several 'buffer companies' until a 'broker' buys the goods, sells them on to another EU company, and reclaims the VAT. The process may be completed in days or even hours. The products are usually small but high value with buoyant markets, eg mobile phones and computer chips. This fraud can also be perpetrated simply with paperwork (ie there may be no physical products involved). The stolen VAT disappears with the company, thus the 'missing trader'. An example of this type of fraud is set out below.

Figure 9.2 Example of carousel fraud

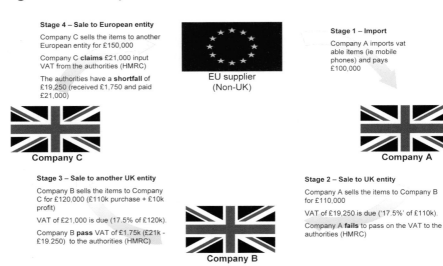

Companies may be active in more than one chain simultaneously.

9.4 Bank fraud and identity theft

Banks are natural targets for organised crime as they are sources of valuable data as well as money.

9.4.1   A variety of card frauds

Figures from the UK Association of Payment and Clearing Services (APACS) show losses from credit and debit card fraud growing five-fold since the mid-1990s and reaching £440 million in 2007. Seventy-five per cent of this may be due to organised attacks.

SOCA reports that serious organised criminals are also involved in taking over bank accounts and withdrawing funds, or opening new accounts under false names, drawing on credit and then disappearing. There has also been an increase in mortgage and cheque frauds (including counterfeit cheques).

Much of the diversification has been prompted by the introduction of 'Chip and PIN' which has made card cloning more difficult. Another response can be seen in the sharp rise in so-called "card-not-present" fraud, when card details are used to buy goods online, by phone or via mail order. More frauds are also being committed overseas by criminals using stolen UK card details. Fraud committed abroad now accounts for more than £200 million of the UK total, and APACS is trying to encourage other countries to implement chip and PIN-style regimes in order to make this type of crime more difficult.

9.4.2   The growth of identity theft

Identity fraud has always been a major tool of organised crime but recent years have seen a change of emphasis with implications for almost every type of business. The prime target is personal data. Fraudulently acquired identities are used to access databases and obtain credit, loans and goods. The global cost runs into billions of pounds.

Confidential details on individuals and companies is obtained through a variety of means such as outright data theft, attacks on company information systems and 'social engineering' (where criminals seek to coerce employees into giving them information, usually customer details).

Freelance hackers sell organised criminals illegally obtained customer lists and bank details plus advanced hacking software which can be used for the same purpose. The majority of malicious software ('malware') is designed to obtain credit card details, bank account details, passwords and PIN numbers, or to create large networks of infected computers ('botnets'), which can be controlled remotely and used to steal IDs and attack websites. A successful attack on a big bank or retailer can provide the details needed to create thousands of fraudulent identities.

'Phishing' is perhaps the best-known form of internet attack. Bulk e-mailings are sent purporting to be from a bank. The aim is to attract victims to a lookalike website where they can be tricked into disclosing their bank details. Because such e-mails are sent in huge numbers even a small number of 'catches' can make the exercise a profitable one. Hi-tech criminals also obtain data from online gaming, recruitment and social networking sites in order to make the e-mails look credible. Such attacks have aimed increasingly at the customers of smaller financial institutions, eg credit unions and small banks where there is often a lack of staff and resources with which to counter the threat.

In 2007 APACS was aware of 25,796 bogus websites in the UK alone, up from 14,156 in 2006. Gartner Inc. reported that $3.2 billion was lost to phishing attacks in the US in the 12 months to August 2007. It estimated that about 57 million Americans received a phishing email in 2007.

9.5   The danger of infiltration

Organised criminals look continually for weaknesses in corporate procedures, systems and personnel. The threat is not just an external one. Britain's National Criminal Intelligence Service (NCIS) reported in September 2005 that 'serious organised criminals set out to infiltrate target companies, looking to place individuals in positions where they have access to money, goods, or information that can be turned to financial gain'. Banks and other financial institutions are particularly at risk and there have also been numerous cases of staff being bribed and blackmailed into helping gangs.

9.6   Damaging corporate reputations

Even the suspicion of identity theft can do crushing damage to organisational reputations and those of their top executives. The Chairman of HM Revenue and Customs (HMRC) resigned in early 2008 after two computer discs holding the personal details of all families with a child under 16 (including 25 million people's bank details) went missing.

The UK Financial Services Authority (FSA) has fined major financial institutions for not having appropriate systems and controls for protecting customer data. In one case fraudsters had used publicly available information to impersonate customers and obtain policy and bank account details from an insurer's call centre. The fraudsters then used this information to request the surrender of policies worth over £3 million.

9.7 Money laundering: compromising legitimate businesses

There is little point in gangs 'earning' large profits unless they can be spent with minimal risk of detection. Moreover, as the FSA points out, organised crime 'needs access to the financial system much the same as a legitimate business does'. The British government estimates that £25 billion is laundered in the UK each year and the sums involved globally run into hundreds of billions. The money is passed through legitimate outlets or mixed with legitimate funds in order to disguise its source.

Cash remains the mainstay of criminal funds. It leaves no audit trail and is highly flexible. Countries where cash is still the mainstay of the economy are particularly vulnerable, as are cash-dominated companies (such as those in property and entertainment) in any country. Laundered funds are poured into a range of investments, including criminal-owned companies, and often held in the names of relatives, associates, or 'gatekeepers'. Cash is also smuggled abroad using Alternative Remittance Systems (ARS), otherwise known as underground banking, via money transmission agents (MTAs) who act like private bankers, accepting deposits and making payments.

Money laundering risks tainting businesses by association with criminal funds and opens management to blackmail once such funds have been accepted, however innocently. Legitimate businesses are then used to provide cover for criminal activity by facilitating illicit trades.

Criminals also target solicitors, accountants and other professionals with access to the financial sector and the expertise to integrate 'dirty' money into the financial system. Professional help may be witting or unwitting, and in some cases is the result of coercion.

9.8 Reducing the risk

If this account of organised crime seems daunting it should be remembered that the gangs have often been foiled when institutions have made a concerted effort. British online banking fraud losses fell by 33 per cent in 2006, partly as a result of greater public awareness of 'phishing' scams. Anti-fraud measures, including intelligence-led detection and more rigorous checks, have halved overall welfare fraud losses since 2001.

Chapter 10 describes a range of anti-fraud measures, but those particularly relevant to deterring organised crime are outlined briefly here.

9.8.1 Due diligence

In-depth, accurate and timely information allows companies to make informed decisions regarding who they are, or may be, doing business with and enables them to take necessary precautions for monitoring high-risk areas of operation. Due diligence involves the search, collection and analysis of information from both public sources (court cases, press reports, credit checks, etc.) and confidential sources on the background, ownership, business track record, reputation and integrity of entities or individuals. Those doing business in states suffering high levels of corruption should consider using investigators from outside the country concerned.

9.8.2 Recruitment screening

Fraudsters and their stooges can be stopped from entering the workplace if new recruits – including temporary and contract staff – are properly vetted. It is also essential to prevent staff from being corrupted or intimidated for example by encouraging to raise any issues with line management or HR and requiring applicants to undertake interviews with a second person, where appropriate. The recruitment processes of a business need to be thorough, particularly where appointing people to positions of trust. Ongoing monitoring of activity must be undertaken: if a person's lifestyle appears to be different to their known salary it is best to start thinking about where they get their money from.

9.8.3 Transaction analysis

'Know your customer' (KYC) measures such as account profiling provides some protection for banks. Many businesses now go further and use detection fraud software. This triggers alerts if activities in a customer's account fall outside given parameters. Alerts are then prioritised for review by fraud analysts who evaluate unusual factors (eg similar names with different addresses and atypical spending patterns) and contact customers. Of course even the best software is no substitute for well-trained and vigilant staff.

9.8.4 Ensuring data protection discipline

Data theft can be prevented by a comprehensive and coherent series of steps.

1. Promulgating a clear and easily accessible data protection policy.

2. Implementing an effective compliance programme with annual sign-off for all managers and staff.

10.2   Governance

There are several aspects to good corporate governance on fraud issues:

- leadership;

- strategic direction;

- culture and ethics;

- defined roles and responsibilities;

- approval of key anti-fraud policies;

- establishing the role of governance units; and

- interaction with executive and oversight committees.

Firm commitment and clear direction from a company's leaders is essential to any successful anti-fraud programme. Though individual functions and business units can often take useful steps, only the board and senior managers can define and approve a comprehensive strategy. Of course, the detailed formulation of the strategy should be delegated to those within the organisation with the expertise to devise and execute it.

The challenge for some businesses is how to get this level of commitment from senior management. Those who can initiate or help drive through the programme include the following.

1. Executive directors who are keen to maintain or enhance the integrity of the firm.

2. Audit and/or risk committees who are able to challenge management about minimising the risk of fraud, theft and inappropriate conduct.

3. Shareholders who can stop investing in companies failing to prevent fraud-driven value erosion.

4. Managers in governance functions such as internal audit, risk, compliance and anti-fraud units.

5. Senior management who are keen to stop the erosion of assets and integrity of their area of business.

10.2.1   Setting examples

Leadership is about more than collective responsibility, it has a personal aspect too. Surveys confirm that staff pay far more attention to what their bosses do than to what they say. Individual directors and senior managers need to set good examples not only in areas such as expenses claims and personal use of company facilities, but also in clear compliance with anti-fraud procedures.

A LEAD FROM THE TOP?

A major company arranged for a fraud awareness training course in one of their overseas businesses. It became clear that no expatriate managers from the British or American HQs would attend. Local employees complained this implied that: (a) locals were more likely to commit fraud or engage in corruption; and (b) that the expatriates saw themselves as above suspicion. Neither assumption was true, but these perceptions damaged efforts to build support for the anti-fraud programme.

10.2.2 The chain of responsibility

Each top layer of the business has a crucial role to play.

1. The *chief executive* should lead by example, allocating sufficient resources to anti-fraud efforts and holding senior management accountable for compliance violations.

2. *Senior management* must have a clear view of what is needed to prevent, detect and respond to fraud. They must then create a comprehensive fraud management strategy for approval by the board.

3. It is not only essential that the *chairman and board* show open and active support for the anti-fraud strategy, they must also review its effectiveness via a regular agenda item.

4. The board may delegate detailed oversight to *the audit and/or risk committee,* tasking it with reviewing and discussing issues with auditors and other interested parties (the board and/or audit committee may require training in order to accurately assess the materials they will need to see).

5. *Department or function heads* should ensure day-to-day implementation of the strategy in their areas.

6. *A single senior manager* should be given authority to coordinate all fraud risk management activities, plus responsibility for delivering the strategy across the organisation (this person is sometimes referred to as the fraud control officer, head of fraud or head of financial crime).

   He or she will benefit from the support of a *committee of cross-functional managers* which should:

   (a) coordinate the organisation's fraud risk assessment efforts;
   (b) oversee the precise design and implementation of anti-fraud measures; and
   (c) report regularly to the board and/or audit committee.

10.2.3 Devising a strategy

A clear anti-fraud strategy facilitates clear thinking within the organisation and lets all stakeholders know what is expected of them. Clearly a programme with goals matching those of the organisation as a whole is more likely to be a success.

An anti-fraud programme should be proportionate to the level and variety of risks that a business faces as well as to its market status. This will be determined by the sector (and countries) in which it operates, eg accounts manipulation is a bigger risk in listed companies.

Though senior management is unlikely to be involved in anti-fraud initiatives on a daily basis it is critical that they set out the key elements of the anti-fraud strategy to coordinate the various parts of the fraud management programme. Without this the organisation will end up with a set of sporadic and uncoordinated activities with duplication in some areas, lack of key initiatives in others and a general air of confusion.

Setting strategic direction involves setting out the following.

1. The key objectives of the company's anti-fraud arrangements, ie being 'best in class', in line with peer organisations, zero tolerance, etc.

2. An implementation timetable.

3. High-level reporting requirements so that management and other stakeholders are kept informed.

The approval process should involve all main internal stakeholders from the outset in order to minimise disagreements, maximise support and to make the most of their expertise.

Time invested in strategy formulation is invaluable in ensuring that the resulting programme will be truly integrated into the wider organisation. Well thought-out objectives provide a clear mandate for departments and business units, and establish a clear line of responsibility.

10.2.4 Culture and ethics

Ethical attitudes are the main determinants of culture and the basis of fraud prevention. Honesty is vital but it is not enough. In the long run (and often in the shorter term too) an organisation is judged by how it treats people. Corporate values express themselves in how the company deals with employees, customers, suppliers and others.

An ethical culture helps prevent fraud by promoting clarity about right and wrong. And by operating fairly a company maximises staff loyalty, making employees allies in fraud prevention.

Appropriate corporate behaviour can be encouraged through a range of actions including the following.

1. Promulgating a statement of ethical principles for the business.

2. Ensuring all staff are made aware of these principles via training, internal publicity and the induction process.

3. Establishing appropriate oversight and disciplinary processes.

The Board should discuss the relevance of the principles on a periodic basis and this should include consideration of whether in practice, management and staff are aware of and abide by these principles.

10.2.5 Ending unnecessary pressure

Pressure to deliver unreasonable targets and ill-considered incentives help to cause fraud. In such cases management is unwittingly incentivising staff to focus obsessively on narrow self-interest at the expense of the company.

Every level of management needs to ask itself the following questions.

1. What pressures are people under in the company?

2. Are management unwittingly creating pressures that will lead people to manipulate data in order to protect themselves?

3. Is the pressure making people resentful? Is it making them care less about the company's interests?

4. Where are the pressure points?

5. Which pressures are intrinsic and which are unnecessary?

6. What is an acceptable level of pressure?

7. Where do people go if they have a concern and are these mechanisms effective in helping resolve or managing these pressures?

10.2.6 Promoting openness

Fraud becomes easier in a non-transparent business environment. Three steps are essential to ensure a culture of openness.

1. Those charged with risk assessment and financial probity must have

full and timely access both to relevant data and those responsible for operating controls.

2. Managers and executives right up to board level must be willing to hear bad news without 'shooting the messenger' or pressurising colleagues to provide positive reports regardless of underlying facts. Staff must be assured of protection if they 'blow the whistle' on suspected fraud.

3. Responsible criticism and proper professional scepticism must be valued rather than being dismissed as 'negativity'. A questioning frame of mind helps to expose gaps in corporate defences.

10.2.7 Codes of conduct

A code of conduct helps to assert the standards that define acceptable behaviour in the workplace. It sets the cultural tone and raises awareness of the leadership's commitment to integrity and ethical conduct.

A corporate code of ethics should do the following.

1. Emphasise the need for everyone in the organisation to take personal responsibility for their own behaviour.

2. Be tailored to the company's culture and management style. There must be no question of simply copying another company's policies.

3. Be clear, concise and unambiguous. Staff should find it easy to understand and absorb the key points.

4. Be supported by realistic examples and constructive practical guidance on a function-by-function basis.

5. Be regularly refreshed and updated.

6. Be supported by regular and prominent internal publicity.

An organisation should consider using focus groups to ensure that a draft code is user friendly.

10.2.8 Employee attitude surveys

Independently conducted surveys can reveal how the corporate culture is seen by those working within it. The results can be unsettling, though this makes them all the more valuable. The following are the results from the *The KPMG in the US Integrity Survey 2005/06* which analysed the US workforce:

1. Fifty-two per cent felt their employer's code of conduct was not taken seriously.

2. Forty-nine per cent believed they would be rewarded according to results rather than the means used to achieve them.

3. Fifty-five per cent reported that they lacked understanding of the standards that applied to their jobs.

Attitude surveys are also useful in gauging employee awareness of anti-fraud policies and procedures. More sophisticated interviewing skills and focus groups may be needed to tease out details of staff concerns and underlying attitudes. One such tool is an integrity survey. This usually involves a number of confidential questionnaires probing relationships between perceived conduct and the organisation's ethical climate. The results are used to prepare a detailed 'integrity profile'.

10.2.9 Substance over form

A company wanted to see how effective its fraud awareness had been. It commissioned a survey of several hundred employees. Questions included the following:

1. What in your opinion is the extent of fraud (if any) in your area of the company?

2. If you suspected fraud in the last year, did you report it?

3. If you reported your suspicions, which of the following did you report this through?

    (a) Internal audit.
    (b) Ethics reporting line.
    (c) Management.
    (d) A work colleague.
    (e) Someone outside the company.

4. If you reported suspected fraud, were you satisfied with the company's response?

5. Which methods do you prefer for providing information about fraud prevention?

    (a) Face-to-face training.
    (b) Team meetings.
    (c) Intranet.
    (d) Booklet or written information.
    (e) E-mail alerts.

The survey found that respondents favoured reporting their suspicions to line managers; that a large minority had not received fraud training; and that the majority believed tailored training was the most effective way to raise awareness.

10.2.10   Ensuring controls are operating as intended

Executives should ensure there is a robust control oversight function able to challenge management and ensure that controls are relevant and effective. But if this unit is under-skilled, inadequately resourced or lacking a clear sense of purpose or direction it is likely to fail.

10.2.11   Avoiding red tape

Many companies have made the mistake of introducing more and more controls to combat fraud but the truth is that the less bureaucracy, the easier it is to manage risk. The key is to manage risk in ways that enhance business performance, not to be obsessed with it and over-controlled, or ignorant and unduly exposed.

Management are likely to define success fairly narrowly, in cost/benefit terms. Employees are likely to have a different perspective: has the programme made working life more difficult? Has it eroded trust within the company? Does it feel as if staff are all under suspicion? Great care must be taken to consider these valid concerns. An undercurrent of hostility to management is utterly counter-productive; indeed, an over-focus on detailed rules can lead to an unthinking 'compliance culture' where the 'letter of the law' trumps serious analysis and judgement.

10.3   Operations

A set of coordinated activities are required for effective fraud identification, prevention, detection and response. Key activities can be summarised as follows.

1. Reporting arrangements:

    (a) internal and external reporting requirements including escalation procedures;
    (b) mechanisms to report/log potential fraud risks and control weaknesses; and
    (c) periodic collation of fraud loss and fraud risk information.

2. Preparing anti-fraud policies, procedures and guidelines for management review.

3. Determining the applicability of business' operational risk methodology to the assessment of fraud risk.

4. Whistleblowing arrangements.

5. Fraud response plans.

6. Investigation guidelines.

7. The use of data analytics and other forms of review to identify unusual activity which may indicate fraud or other forms of impropriety.

8. Understanding the history and extent of fraud loss.

9. Establishing a group, attended by key contributors, such as a fraud forum to discuss issues, review indicators and develop initiatives. Attendees should include the heads of fraud, information security (taking into account both technology and document information), human resources, internal audit, anti-money laundering, and representatives from the operational business units.

10. Intelligence gathering – understanding threats in the industry and potential mitigation measures. This information can be fed into the fraud forum.

11. Ensure that anti-fraud initiatives align with IT security initiatives.

12. Employee and third-party due diligence.

13. Establishing key performance indicators (KPIs) and key risk indicators (KRIs).

14. Ensuring there are sufficiently skilled internal and external resources available as part of a proportionate response.

> **LEFT FOOT, RIGHT FOOT**
>
> Individual business units in a large company had their own anti-fraud policies and initiatives. Problems arose because there were also different policies for recording fraud losses in the accounts and while some required staff to report suspicions, others left this to individual discretion. Inevitably this led to confusion as to the true cost of fraud to the group.

10.3.1 Mechanisms for reporting misconduct

Tip-offs are one of the more common methods of fraud detection and most are from employees. Internal reporting channels should be widely publicised. Staff should be encouraged to express concerns via line management, but an independent 'hotline' should also be set up to provide them with a greater sense of security as well as ensuring a more consistent response to callers. A well-designed hotline ensures that concerns are reported through on a 'no names' basis (though many of those who use them are in fact ready to give their name and other details).

Consistent protocols are needed to sift reports and determine how they will be handled. Qualified individuals (from internal audit, legal, security, etc.) should determine whether the substance of an allegation could trigger a financial reporting risk. Criteria are needed to determine which allegations are escalated to the audit committee. It is important to follow up periodically with employees after the case has been closed to ensure that they have not experienced any retaliation. Data should be collated in a consistent manner and sent to a central repository.

10.3.2 Response

When significant fraud is detected swift and decisive action is required. A fraud response plan minimises confusion, cuts debate on what to do and provides options. When the response stage is complete, the organisation should ensure that lessons are captured and acted on. This will almost certainly mean modification of its control systems.

The basis of any effective response plan is to ensure that some simple questions are always asked and answered early in the process.

1. When did the fraud start?

2. Why did the fraudster(s) do it?

3. Were there warning signs and did we ignore them?

4. Were third parties involved?

5. What is the full extent of our loss?

6. Which controls failed, or were not in place?

7. What actions are we taking to stop a repetition?

10.3.3 Fraud risk methodology

A business needs to ensure that fraud risks are identified, controls matched and their effectiveness checked through rigorous challenge, and mitigation is effective and proportionate. Most businesses have operational risk methodologies and they should consider whether these would be appropriate bases for carrying out the assessment of fraud risks. The following factors should be considered.

1. Can fraud risks be clearly defined and documented?

2. Will sufficient detail on controls be captured?

3. Is there a logical and consistent process for assessing and classifying control effectiveness?

4. Is there a process in place to individually rate the likelihood of occurrence and impact of the risk should it occur?

5. Can proposed risk mitigation actions be documented within the assessment?

6. Can ownership for taking specific risk mitigation be attributed to individuals in the firm?

PAYING THE PRICE

Britain's financial regulators fined a major company £300,000 for poor anti-fraud controls. The company carried out investment trades for its clients, using highly sensitive personal data in the process. Staff were able to manipulate client identities and account information in order to process unauthorised trades. Fraudulent payments totalled over £300,000.

10.3.4 Enforcement and accountability

A consistent, transparent and credible disciplinary process sends a powerful message that fraud is taken seriously. Discipline must be applied consistently, regardless of rank, tenure or function.

Managers should be disciplined in the following instances.

1. When they knew, or should have known, that fraud might be occurring.

2. When they directed or pressured others to violate company standards to meet business objectives, or set unrealistic goals that had the same effect.

3. When they had a prior history of missing or permitting violations.

4. When they retaliated against others for reporting concerns.

10.3.5 Recruitment screening

Staff fraud shatters trust and sows disturbing seeds of doubt: how far back does it go? How far has it gone? Who exactly is involved? And because it is an inside job, the fraud can have a devastating impact on a company's reputation.

The first line of defence against internal fraud is to prevent fraudsters from entering the workplace. HR teams have an essential part to play by ensuring that new recruits are properly vetted and their qualifications and employment histories verified. Yet screening is often a low priority with checks left entirely to the individual recruiter. Those carried out on prospective staff are invariably weaker than for prospective clients and customers.

A GLOWING TRIBUTE

An employee of a betting company obtained his job partly as a result of glowing references. He subsequently manipulated internal approval thresholds and entered into a number of unauthorised transactions losing over half a million pounds. It turned out that the references were from his wife, issued under her maiden name. Embarrassingly, management of the company had contacted her (not knowing the relationship) to check the reference but had not sought to confirm her relationship to the employee (and now the convicted fraudster).

10.3.6 Checking the applicant's claims

Many fraud cases involve a lie or inconsistency, either on the fraudster's job application or during interview. The following methods will prove helpful in assessing those seeking a position of trust.

1. Ask to see a passport or other appropriate document in order to verify the applicant's identity.

2. Check qualifications against up-to-date professional membership registers (which can often be done by telephone and for nothing) or other publicly available databases.

3. Check whether the applicant actually went to the places of higher education listed on his CV.

4. Probe gaps in a career history and ask why the applicant left previous jobs.

5. Contact referees personally and by telephone. Obtain telephone numbers independently rather than relying on the candidate. Ascertain the referee's position in their organisation.

6. Beware of name dropping on CVs or at interviews; ask questions about work supposedly done for well-known companies or clients.

HAT TRICK

A credit controller committed the same fraud at three companies in succession. She claimed to be a qualified chartered accountant but had never taken an accountancy exam. Indeed, she had spent time in jail between jobs. None of the companies enquired whether she was listed on The Institute of Chartered Accountants' register of members. The check is free, can be done by telephone in less than two minutes and would have saved these companies a total of £800,000.

Temporary employees should not be entrusted with valuable assets (including data). Unquestioning and sometimes undeserved confidence is often placed in companies supplying such staff. Companies should ensure that recruitment agencies' screening procedures are consistent with their own. Similar risks arise with contract staff.

> **THE GANGSTER'S GIRLFRIEND**
>
> A company employed a temporary bought ledger clerk. Unfortunately her boyfriend belonged to a cheque fraud gang which had systematically placed her in a series of businesses. The company became aware of the fraud when the police arrested gang members on an unrelated matter. Two of the company's cheques were found in their pockets.

10.3.7   Scrutinising staff

Trust is essential to the effective workings of any organisation, but it should not be blind or unthinking. Many frauds occur because companies refuse to consider that employees, particularly older or senior ones, might be dishonest. Once again, a few straightforward procedures can help to prevent fraud.

10.3.8   Prior business relationships

It is best to be aware if staff undertaking significant duties have worked together at a former employer. Such situations can lead to collusion, eg managers have recruited old colleagues, and even whole teams, for that very purpose.

10.3.9   Monitoring holidays and work patterns

A simple but effective anti-fraud measure is to require all staff in sensitive positions to take at least two weeks continuous holiday a year and monitor that this actually happens. A significant number of frauds come to light during such periods of absence. Workaholics and staff working unusual hours, eg at weekends especially those that have not been putting in regular hours during the week, should be monitored.

10.3.10   Red flags

Indicators of potential fraud are often referred to as 'red flags'. Monitoring these indicators can help direct enquiries to specific areas or activities within the business and reduce the time that fraud may go undetected. Examples of red flags include:

- refusing to take annual leave;

- undeclared criminal records;

- alteration of customer details;

- complaints of misconduct;
- accounts not reconciling;
- staff living beyond their means;
- expense claim abnormalities and missing receipts; and
- unsubmitted reports.

10.3.11 Third-party due diligence

Due diligence should also be undertaken on third parties such as acquisition targets, investors, joint-venture partners, suppliers and agents before a business relationship begins. A small investment of time and money before a contract is signed may prevent large monetary and reputational losses afterwards. If a company lacks the skills or time for such checks it can draw on any number of specialist providers of corporate intelligence services.

A DANGEROUS LIAISON AVOIDED

An international development bank was considering a long-term loan to a privately owned company in western Asia. Following a detailed investigation, which included research in public records and local enquiries, information was uncovered which cast doubt on the probity and suitability of the prospective partners, including allegations of serious crime. It was also discovered that much of the documentation submitted to the bank was false and that the company had been blacklisted by its own national regulatory authorities. The bank withdrew from the project.

10.3.12 The emergence of data analytics

Many indicators of actual or potential fraud sit within an organisation's financial, operational and transactional data. Data analytic technology enables enormous volumes of information to be processed quickly and combed for trends and/or anomalous events. It enhances the fraud risk profile and aids detection of fraud by leveraging hitherto unexploited internal knowledge.

Data analytics have been particularly effective in uncovering multiple fraudulent insurance claims by colluding individuals. It can also be used to analyse financial system data, eg by reviewing times during the day when journals are posted.

Transactions can be analysed using either retrospective or continuous monitoring. The latter allows an organisation to identify potentially fraudulent transactions on a daily, weekly or monthly basis.

Organisations frequently use continuous monitoring to focus on narrow bands of transactions and areas posing particularly strong risks.

10.3.13   Understanding the extent of fraud losses

Organisations need to collate data on fraud incidents and loss. Two problems usually arise. Firstly, that data is not recorded and measured consistently and collated at a central point. Secondly, that all frauds occurring within or being perpetrated on the business are not being identified. Organisations need to ensure a rigorous approach is adopted to identify fraud incidents and hence loss.

Selecting sample information and undertaking a forensic review of all items in the sample is one way to obtain an understanding of the problem. As an example, a sample of invoices for particular months could be collated and each examined to detect suspect, unusual or clearly fraudulent content such as duplicate amounts or invoices with different reference numbers but requesting payment for work previously invoiced and paid. This analysis, provided it is undertaken on a logical and preferably statistical basis, may tell us something about the potential extent of fraud loss and may, provided it is a statistically sound sample be applied to the population. Accompanying this approach should be a clearly defined reporting process that ensures consistent measurement and reporting, followed by appropriate analysis.

This type of approach enables organisations to make more informed decisions on:

(a) the extent and impact of fraud losses; and

(b) the type and extent of actions to address and reduce fraud.

10.3.14   Structuring investigations

When information on an actual or potential fraud comes to light, management should be prepared to conduct a comprehensive and objective internal investigation. Investigations should follow a clear procedure to ensure the facts are identified, evidence and assets secured, and that no further loss occurs. There are many issues to address.

1. Developing a clear understanding of the fraud, or allegations, and their implications.

2. Identifying the investigative skills and investigators required.

3. Confidentiality and security.

4. Identifying sources of information and potential evidence.

5. Evidence handling and documentation.

6. Interview processes.

7. IT needs, including restricting access to, and imaging from, computers.

8. Identifying and agreeing recovery actions.

9. Reporting to the authorities.

Investigations must be conducted in a robust, professional and fair manner. The organisation will need to ensure either that it has adequately trained internal resources to undertake the investigation, or that it engages properly qualified external advisers. As fraud investigations often require specialist skills and the use of sophisticated forensic technology techniques, many organisations recognise that they cannot keep all of the necessary resources in-house.

A well-designed investigative process will typically include the following features.

1. Oversight by the audit committee, or a special committee of the Board, either of which must be comprised of independent directors who are able to ward off undue pressure and interference from management.

2. Senior internal staff allocated to the investigation, eg the head of fraud or internal audit. External fraud examiners should not be left unsupervised.

3. Vetting by the organisation's external auditor so that it can rely upon the proposed scope of work when reviewing financial statements.

4. Full cooperation requirements for staff including data preservation undertakings. No rank-and-file employee, let alone managers, can be allowed to obscure the facts.

5. Reporting protocols, providing the external auditors, regulators and (where appropriate) the media with information about the investigation's findings.

10.3.15 Interviewing: a neglected skill

Figure 10.2 Listening to what people say

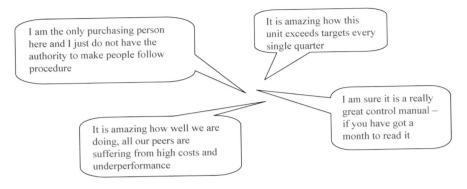

The above comments were made during the first few minutes of a meeting with a financial controller. Such remarks provide valuable pointers to how someone feels about his job and perhaps the state of the company he works for.

Effective interviewing and counselling are key management skills and should be part of executive fraud awareness training. Appraisals can be used to identify staff concerns, morale problems and questionable management styles. Managers need to be able to ask questions in an unthreatening yet challenging way. Sometimes staff signal concerns rather than stating them outright and managers must learn how to recognise such signs. The necessary skills are best developed using interview simulations based on realistic scenarios.

10.4   Risk

Identification, assessment and management of internal and external fraud risks are some of the most effective weapons in the fight against fraud. Information about systems and policy weaknesses has huge medium- and long-term value. If all an organisation is doing is detecting, investigating and punishing fraud, it is merely generating activity rather than ensuring the outcome which matters most – reduced losses.

Management should ensure that regular and comprehensive risk assessment is conducted across the entire organisation. This should do more than consider significant business units, processes, and accounts; it is also vital to study the underlying reality of internal relationships and the quality of key indicators.

This approach can often be resource-intensive and this underlines the need for genuine high-level commitment to fraud risk management.

10.4.1 Risk profiling

Fraud risk profiling is a proven process which enables a company to develop a detailed understanding of the specific dangers it faces. This in turn provides a basis on which to challenge the quality of existing controls.

Risk profiling should not be carried out in isolation: it is important to benchmark against competitors and incorporate lessons from the marketplace. It is also helpful to get advice from experienced fraud investigation and risk-management specialists.

Fraud usually involves manipulating an internal process, so understanding fraud risks also means getting to know an organisation's key processes, eg sales, stock, purchasing. Each key process should be profiled for fraud risk. Figure 10.3 shows those often found in the purchase-to-pay process.

Figure 10.3 Identifying specific risks in the process

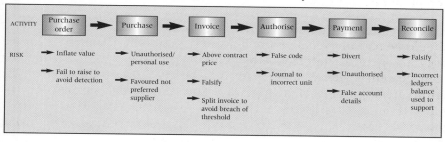

10.4.2 Fraud risk assessment

Mapping the key risks is the first important step. It is then necessary to assess:

- what internal and external relationships could impact the business;

- how key decisions are made during these relationships and by whom; and

- how the decision-making process could be manipulated through fraud.

Figure 10.4 Profiling and assessing fraud risk

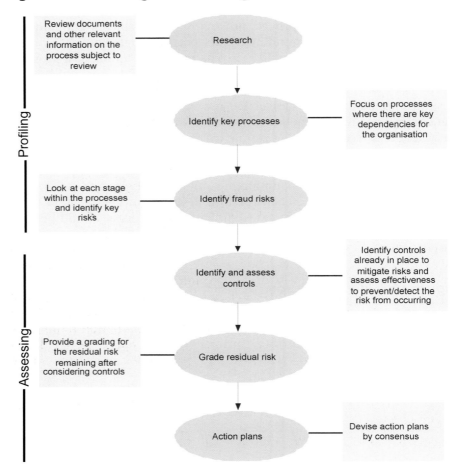

10.4.3   Risk assessment methodology

The next stage is to agree a risk assessment methodology and ensure it is used consistently. Risks can then be matched with existing controls by charting them alongside the main stages of the relevant business process. An example is set out in figure 10.5.

Figure 10.5 Matching fraud risks with controls and performance measures

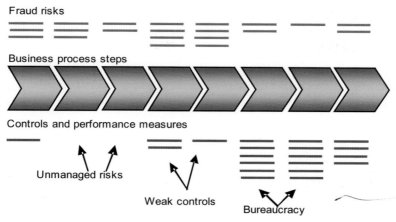

Risks should be graded according to impact and likelihood. A simple 1 to 5 rating classification can be used to rate both likelihood and impact. These ratings can then be used to determine the overall residual risk rating. For example, a risk assessed as having a likelihood rating of 2 (low) and an impact rating of 4 (high), would have an overall residual risk rating of 10. Management then needs to decide whether to mitigate the risk by introducing further controls or to accept it. Detailed and timetabled action plans with clear accountabilities will have to be devised to address control weaknesses.

Table 10.1 illustrates how the resulting assessment of a fraud risk may be recorded.

Table 10.1 Fraud risk assessment

No.	Fraud risk	Controls	Likelihood	Impact	Rating	Mitigation actions
1	The risk that the accounts receivable staff embezzle customer payments	• All mail is opened by clerk and placed in tray. • Cash and other deposits are recorded in the system by data entry staff. • Daily review of cash receipts.	Low	Medium	Moderate	• Supervisor to oversee mail opening and recording of receipts. • Daily cash reconciliation. • Reinforce company fraud policy and reporting suspected unusual activity. • Client queries to be handled in Operations rather than Receivables.

10.4.4 Finding risk in wider organisational issues

Companies should probe beyond the risks inherent in technical processes and examine the underlying realities of organisational life. The following questions should help.

1. What is the quality of the strategic management process? The lack of a comprehensive strategy can encourage personal and business unit agendas at the expense of focusing on key risks.

2. What are the real dynamics of internal control? Are roles and accountabilities uncertain or ignored? Do some staff have power well beyond their formal position in the hierarchy?

3. Are project teams and business units properly trained and staffed to fulfil the financial and procurement roles that have been devolved to them?

4. Does the finance department have the high-level support it needs to deter and detect fraud? If this is not provided other functions will seek greater independence and develop their own, usually less rigorous, practises.

5. What is the likely impact of reward structures? Do bonus and earn-out arrangements risk creating perverse incentives?

6. What is the underlying quality of the performance measures on which risk management relies?

7. Are controls actually implemented? A finance department may log a purchase order but does the financial controller check to see if it has been approved by the appropriate person? Or that costs are within agreed parameters?

8. What is the actual level of risk awareness? All of the controls in the world will fail if staff, particularly managers, do not take fraud risk seriously enough.

10.5 Training and awareness

A good anti-fraud programme creates a structure in which opportunity to commit fraud is minimised. Deterrence relies on potential fraudsters seeing the strength of arrangements to prevent, detect, investigate and punish fraud.

10.5.1 Fraud awareness and training

Staff can be a bulwark against fraud if they know how to spot it, appreciate how damaging it can be, and are willing to report their suspicions. But it needs focused and continuing training, plus high-profile internal publicity, to mobilise the honest majority to actively protect their organisation's reputation, budget and cash flows.

Fraud awareness and training needs two further objectives: the development of an effective anti-fraud culture that works, and the creation of a strong deterrent effect. In the former case, the aim should be to build staff confidence in the counter-fraud effort, its importance and prospects for success. In the latter case, the aim should be to convince prospective fraudsters that the risks of being caught or discovered as a result of perpetrating fraud are too high.

Specific steps are as follows.

1. Inform staff that the business will not tolerate fraud (sometimes referred to as 'zero tolerance') and request their cooperation by reporting suspicions to the appropriate (nominated) person.

2. Help staff understand the tangible problems arising from fraud and the benefits that will flow from reducing fraud losses (for instance in releasing funding for better systems or higher remuneration).

3. Educate staff in the risks arising from different business processes. Controls often seem bureaucratic and burdensome because staff are not told the reasoning behind them.

4. Train staff to identify and help mitigate fraud risk. It is also important to brief them on any obligations that the business may have to report suspected instances of fraud and potential fraud risks, for example, to regulators.

5. Training should be planned around specific job functions and risk areas. Staff also need practical guidance on the warning signs, issues and ethical dilemmas they might face in their jobs. When staff attend training sessions, case studies are a useful way of getting them to participate in identifying suspected fraud and escalating reporting.

6. Tailored training should be provided for senior management, staff involved in control functions and those allowed to initiate, approve or account for transactions.

7. Awareness needs to be refreshed at least annually and records should be kept of those receiving training.

8. Key messages need to be reinforced continuously via newsletters, posters, wallet cards and screen savers, as well as team meetings and intranet sites.

Face-to-face tailored training is often the most effective method, but online and other methods can also be successful if designed to engage individual attention.

Typical elements of a training session include:

- defining fraud;

- examples of different types of fraud;

- fraud's impact on the business, individual staff and society;

- fraudster profiles;

- preventing and detecting fraud in the business;

- reporting; and

- case studies.

10.6 Monitoring

Monitoring can provide assurance as to the effectiveness of anti-fraud arrangements and help detect fraudulent activity. It has two elements.

1. *Evaluating the framework*. This includes determining the following:

    (a) Is the framework appropriate to businesses needs?
    (b) Are responses proportionate?
    (c) Are fraud losses and costs recorded and if so, on a consistent basis?
    (d) Has fraud awareness training been effective?
    (e) Are the business units sharing lessons learnt?
    (f) Is there a truly coordinated set of responses to fraud?

    Key indicators are a useful way of determining effectiveness.

2. *Monitoring key fraud risks* requires relevant and readily available data. System-based solutions can be particularly useful, though careful data category selection criteria are required if monitoring staff are not to be swamped with information.

It is important to measure fraud costs in a consistent way. Different parts of the business may write off losses in different ways. This makes it difficult to establish true costs and to compare impacts across the company (see 10.3.13 for details of how to approach the measurement and reporting of fraud loss).

Britain's FSA has noted that 'if fraud losses are "hidden" within other costs, such as bad debts and insurance claims, the underlying causes (and costs) of fraud will be unclear and management will not be in a position to change processes or allocate resources to directly mitigate the risk.' (From the FSA paper firm's high level management of fraud risk, published February 2006).

10.6.1　The importance of clear outcomes

A well-designed programme will incorporate clear criteria for success. There will be a clear set of expected outcomes, against which actual outcomes can be compared. Thought should be given at the planning stage to what indicators will be used for reporting purposes. Then it must be decided how, from where and in what form data is to be gathered and fed back to the owners of the anti-fraud strategy. This mechanism should also be suitable for seeking out, recording and circulating lessons learnt.

10.6.2　A dynamic process

Methods and objectives should not be static. An anti-fraud programme will benefit from incorporating a feedback loop to encourage responses and facilitate ongoing review. If, for instance, the programme is found to make day-to-day operations more onerous for employees, managers will need to be able to react quickly and decisively, either by removing the burden or educating staff about the need for the controls concerned.

10.6.3　Reporting effectively

An effective reporting framework encompasses both KPIs and KRIs. KRIs measure and monitor risks in a proactive way, whereas KPIs measure and monitor the outcomes of the programme.

Examples of KRIs are as follows:

- value at risk by fraud type;

- number of occurrences; and

- new risks identified.

Examples of KPIs are as follows:

- Amount of investment in the programme (including time costs).

- Amount saved by the programme, broken down by loss reduction, recovery of losses and prevention of ongoing losses.

- Number, percentage and level of staff (by function/unit) who have received training.

- Level of staff fraud awareness.

10.6.4 Asking simple questions

Simple methods can complement sophisticated ones. Figure 10.6 provides a short but effective exercise for gaining insight into how a fraud risk-management programme is working. A ranking process, such as 1 to 3 can be used to assess the outcome of each element.

Figure 10.6 Assessing a fraud risk-management programme

Governance and oversight

1. Is there a clearly defined and communicated anti-fraud strategy? ☐
2. Are the key anti-fraud policies well set out and accessible to all staff? ☐
3. Are roles and responsibility for managing fraud risk well defined? ☐
4. Is an annual report circulated to senior management which sets out the cost of fraud on the business, major threats and fraud management initiatives? ☐
5. How clear are reporting channels for reporting suspicions of fraud? ☐
6. Are there clear protections for those reporting fraud? ☐

Operational

7. Is there a yearly review to consider the appropriateness of the business anti-fraud arrangements including resources, funding and acceptable return? ☐
8. Is there a forum for considering the impact and management of fraud and does this include management from the appropriate areas of the business? ☐

Risk assessment

9. How developed is the understanding of fraud risks facing our company? ☐
10. Is there a fraud risk assessment process which requires all business units to identify fraud risks and challenge control effectiveness on a periodic basis? ☐
11. Are fraud risks collated and assessed to determine common characteristics or whether lessons can be shared across the business? ☐
12. How aware of fraud indicators are head office and regional personnel during reviews of numbers of other management information? ☐

Awareness and communication

13. How effective are our recruitment screening procedures at stopping a fraudster joining the company? ☐
14. Is there an annual programme to assess whether staff are aware of their obligations to prevent, detect and report fraud? ☐
15. How aware of fraud indicators are head office and regional personnel during reviews of numbers of other management information? ☐

Monitoring

16. Is there an ongoing assessment as to whether the business anti-fraud arrangements are effective and proportionate to the businesses needs? ☐
17. Are monitoring programmes designed to detect and flag suspected fraud or do they overload people with a large amount of irrelevant information? ☐
18. Is there an annual review to consider the appropriateness of the business anti-fraud arrangements including resources, funding and acceptable return? ☐

Total ☐

10.7 What comes first?

Your company has decided to take a more active stance on fraud. But which activities come first? How can you embed the programme in the business? How do you know if it is having an impact?

10.7.1 Where to start

Planning should start with consideration of two key issues.

1. What is the extent of fraud in the organisation?

2. What are its causes?

The first helps ensure the response is proportionate to business needs. Business units should be asked to collate data on all known frauds so that costs, types and common elements can be centrally evaluated.

Assuming fraud is a real threat, the next step is to consider why it occurs. The fraud triangle (**chapter 3**) sets out the three conditions: opportunity, motivation and rationalisation. It is best to begin with actions which address problems found in the initial assessment. If the losses are a result of bogus expenses, staff failing to work the minimum required hours or a range of low-value indiscretions, they will be best tackled by a fraud awareness programme promoted by top management. The aim should be to deal with the motivational and rationalisation factors.

If fraud is more insidious, eg contract collusion or accounts manipulation, a more sophisticated approach will be required. A combination of awareness programme and implementation of controls aimed at reducing opportunities (eg periodically checking a random sample of transactions and telling staff that this will take place without warning) may be more appropriate.

10.7.2 Embedding an anti-fraud programme

Successful anti-fraud arrangements work because they are embedded in corporate systems. Here are the key measures.

1. Management oversight. Fraud must be a regular agenda item for senior management meetings. The Board and executives need to discuss the company's exposure and response to fraud as well as obtaining reports from business units.

2. Awareness. In addition to fraud training, staff must be reminded periodically of both the company's stance and reporting mechanisms. Business unit managers should provide fraud updates to their teams, supported by messages in internal newsletters and on the intranet.

3. Risk assessment should take place at business unit level with central review of overall weaknesses.

4. Reporting systems should require business units to provide periodic summaries of fraud within their operations. These can be collated

complete, the organisation should ensure that lessons are learnt and acted on.

10.9   Conclusion

We began the book by highlighting the lessons of previous frauds. They are usually disasters waiting to happen, a crystallisation of concealed risk that can be exploited by wilful and organised deception. It is clear that fraud is as a potential factor in every business operation and function.

Preventing fraud also depends on management being aware of its causes. There are always greedy and dishonest people, yet the level of fraud varies from organisation to organisation. Why? Because fraud levels often reflect the wider business environment – culture, ethics, staffing, training, management structures, rewards and communications, as well as the quality of controls. Combating fraud requires the acknowledgement of two unpleasant truths: that needless pressure stimulates dishonesty, and that the worst frauds are usually committed by managers.

Accepting these realities can lead to a business culture based on trust and confidence rather than one of the twin evils of suspicion and complacency. It can also mean a considerable financial return on anti-fraud investment.

Will the nightmare scenario with which the book began apply to your company? Is fraud already draining value from your business? Are you unwittingly creating the conditions in which fraud will thrive? For companies that want to create and keep value, those questions demand urgent answers.

Appendix 1 Further information

KPMG Forensic: www.kpmg.co.uk/services/f/index.cfm

This edition of *Corporate and Financial Fraud* was written by David Lui-jerink, Head of Fraud Risk Management at KPMG Forensic in the UK.

KPMG LLP in the UK is a leading provider of professional services, which include audit, tax, financial and risk advisory. Our Forensic department helps clients reduce reputational risk and commercial loss. We do this by using accounting, investigation, intelligence, technology and industry skills to help clients prevent and resolve commercial disputes, fraud, misconduct and breaches of rules and regulations.

KPMG Forensic also acts in support of law enforcement agencies and other government agencies in civil and criminal investigation cases. This can involve asset tracing, data analytics and giving expert opinion on criminality including fraud and money laundering. With a team of 400 partners and staff across the UK, together with a network of about 2,000 global professionals spanning 31 accredited practices covering 145 countries, we have both a strong national presence and a multinational capability to handle complex cross-border engagements and have undertaken many of the world's largest accounting and financial investigations.

A number of public and private sector organisations also offer helpful information and advice on fraud. Here is a selection of British-based organisations.

Government and regulatory

Financial Services Authority	www.fsa.gov.uk
HM Revenue and Customs	www.hmrc.gov.uk
Information Commissioner	www.ico.gov.uk
NHS Counter Fraud & Security Management Service	www.cfsms.nhs.uk
National Audit Office	www.nao.gov.uk
Intellectual Property Office	www.ipo.gov.uk
Fraud Review	www.attorneygeneral.gov.uk/the_fraud_review_page.htm
Serious Fraud Office	www.sfo.gov.uk

Policing

ACPO Fraud Prevention (Association of Chief Police Officers)	www.acpo.police.uk

City of London Police Economic Crime Unit (designated lead force on fraud for England and Wales)	www.cityoflondon.police.uk/CityPolice/ECD
Metropolitan Police Service	www.met.police.uk/fraudalert
Serious and Organised Crime Agency	www.soca.gov.uk
UK Police Service	www.police.uk

Business and professional

Association of British Insurers	www.abi.org.uk
Association of Certified Fraud Examiners	www.acfeuk.co.uk
Association for Payment Clearing Services	www.apacs.org.uk
Association of Insurance and Risk Managers	www.airmic.com
British Bankers' Association	www.bba.org.uk
Building societies Association	www.bsa.org.uk
The CBI	www.cbi.org.uk
CIFAS – the UK's Fraud Prevention Service	www.cifas.org.uk
Federation of Small Businesses	www.fsb.org.uk
Institute of Counter Fraud Specialists	www.icfs.org.uk
Institute of Business Ethics	www.ibe.org.uk
Institute of Money Laundering Prevention Officers	www.imlpo.com
Insurance Fraud Investigators Group (IFIG)	www.ifig.org

Other advisory bodies

The Fraud Advisory Panel	www.fraudadvisorypanel.org
Public Concern at Work	www.pcaw.co.uk
Eastern Fraud Forum	www.easternfraudforum.co..uk
North East Fraud Forum	www.northeastfraudforum.co.uk
North West Fraud Forum	www.northwestfraudforum.co.uk
London Fraud Forum	www.londonfraudforum.co.uk
South West Fraud Forum	www.southwestfraudforum.co.uk
Yorkshire & Humber Fraud Forum	www.yhff.co.uk
East of Scotland Fraud Forum	www.eastscotlandfraudforum.org.uk
Fraud Women's Network	www.fraudwomensnetwork.com
Midlands Fraud Forum	www.midlandsfraudforum.co.uk

Index